SAP XI Interview Questions, Answers, and Explanations: SAP Exchange Infrastructure Certification Review

By: Terry Sanchez-Clark

SAP XI Interview Questions, Answers, and Explanations: SAP Exchange Infrastructure Certification Review

ISBN 1-933804-68-8
ISBN-13 978-1-933804-68-8

Please visit our website at www.sapcookbook.com

TABLE OF CONTENTS

Introduction:

Almost everyday, IT landscapes of varying degrees are being introduced in the global market. Due to a wide array of software in creating these IT landscapes, the issue of integration among the varied systems has become a problem. Connectivity, differences in format used, and protocols are just some of the requirements which need to be dealt with. Most will want to retain their old system due to the huge volume of data they have accumulated and a translation to a new system means a lot of work. It is not just cost effective to just change an existing system with the one that the market demands. Often times, it will take thousands of dollars, if not millions (for very big companies) to make the shift, and that is just for the change of system. This still does not include the cost to train the required personnel to handle the new system nor is the time involved in the learning process factored in.

An answer to this is the SAP Exchange Infrastructure (SAP XI) component. It is a powerful integration broker that deals with connectivity, format and protocol requirements of various IT landscapes, even with software made by other companies. It supports cross-component business process management (BPM) within the same solution. It is a component of the SAP Netweaver platform and runs on the SAP Web Application Server.

SAP XI provides a common, central repository for different interfaces, therefore reducing the costs of integration and maintenance of IT systems. SAP XI offers and integrated tool set to aid individuals or organizations build their own scenarios by defining messaging interfaces, mappings, routing rules and supports multiple communication approaches like peer to peer connections and central hubs. SAP XI reduces the cost of integration by letting you use existing components such as your investments in electronic data interchange (EDI). SAP XI seamlessly integrates components from both SAP and third-party vendors.

SAP XI offers different prepackaged integration content for different needs. The need to address business contents like data types, message types, interface description, business scenario s, and process patterns are included. SAP XI also offers complete solutions for business problems without compromising the quality that matches industry standards. The SAP XI integration repository is open to third party and custom content, allowing the component to serve as the centralized instance for all integration content. SAP XI allows you to model cross component business processes and scenarios which allows you to control complex business processes across business applications. This covers the full process life cycle, including design, automation, execution, and monitoring. You can even automate processes that will suite your unique need.

For more information, feel free to visit:

www.sap.com/netweaver, www.sap.com/xi, or www.service.sap.com/xi.

Introductory Questions

Question 1: BAPI not found when creating Models

When I create a model in NetWeaver, I can find all the BAPIs that are in the system except the ones I've created.

Can you give me an idea where to find my BAPI ?

A: You need to check "Remote-enabled module", in the attributes for your BAPI/RFC.

Question 2: Transporting XI objects

How do you transport an XI object like the repository or directory to the QA system?

A: You can transport XI objects either by CMS or by file export.

You can go to “Tools”, then “Export objects” and it will be exported as “.tpz” file. You can place the same in the repository_server/import and directory_server/import directory and import it from your QA system.

There is web blog in SDN, which you can visit for more details concerning transporting objects.

https://www.sdn.sap.com/irj/sdn/weblogs?blog=/pub/wlg/2626

Question 3: File not deleted after successful execution

I deleted a file to an IDOC scenario in RWB. After a successful processing, the file was not deleted from the location. This error was displayed:

"Could not delete file 'F:\XIShared\test\1.XML' after processing".

How can I prevent this kind of error from appearing again?

A: You will need to access the properties/permissions for the file you processed. Check if the file is not "read only"in the folder. A "read only" property means that the file can not be deleted so you have to change the setting if it is doable.

Question 4: Messages in HTML Format

I am using a scenario JDBC to file. I don't want the receiver in file format but in HTML format. Also, if I use JDBC to RFC scenario, instead of having the format in RFC, can I have the file in some other format, for example HTML?

A: No. RFC's have to use XML. Remember that your RFC call is going to invoke a function module into an R/3 system and the R/3 system needs to understand the information you are passing. XI only uses and understands XML as its communicating language/medium.

But when sending data outside XI to another application, you can convert this XML payload into any format you want by using adapter modules, content conversion, etc.

Question 5: Mail Package

I am using the Mail Package detailed in a "weblog" to send emails. I want to attach the payload to the email.

Is this possible?

A: Yes it is. You need to use XSLT mapping for this to work.

Question 6: Changing the Name of Datatype

I created a Datatype and saved it. I now need to change the name of the Datatype but it will not allow me to change the name.

Is there a way I can change the name of the Datatype?

A: It is not possible to directly change the name of a datatype.

If you want to preserve the data, then first make a copy of the datatype, and then give the name you want to the copy. Save the copy, and then delete the original data type. You now have "renamed" the datatype.

Question 7: File to File

Can you please explain the steps required completing "File Inbound" and "Outbound" in a local machine (file read from local directory and write into local directory)?

A: You will need to do a lot of reading to understand the topic you are asking. I have made an outline as follows:

Communication channel:

Assigning Communication Channels

http://help.sap.com/saphelp_nw04/helpdata/en/65/b11c409ce22402e10000000a1550b0/frameset.htm

Communication Channel

http://help.sap.com/saphelp_nw04/helpdata/en/2b/d5653fd1d3b81ae10000000a114084/content.htm

Configuring the Sender File/FTP Adapter

http://help.sap.com/saphelp_nw04/helpdata/en/e3/94007075cae04f930cc4c034e411e1/content.htm

Configuring the Receiver File/FTP Adapter

http://help.sap.com/saphelp_nw04/helpdata/en/bc/bb79d6061007419a081e58cbeaaf28/content.htm

Receiver agreement:

Receiver Agreement

http://help.sap.com/saphelp_nw04/helpdata/en/56/02e63f48e58f15e10000000a155106/frameset.htm

Creating a Receiver Agreement

http://help.sap.com/saphelp_nw04/helpdata/en/c1/5194426b44c56ae10000000a155106/frameset.htm

Sender agreement:

Sender Agreement

http://help.sap.com/saphelp_nw04/helpdata/en/db/73e03fc2269615e10000000a155106/frameset.htm

Creating a Sender Agreement

http://help.sap.com/saphelp_nw04/helpdata/en/22/522041cfb7f423e10000000a155106/frameset.htm

For even more detailed information, you can visit the following links.

Introduction to simple (File-XI-File) scenario for Starters (part 1)

https://www.sdn.sap.com/irj/sdn/weblogs?blog=/pub/wlg/1312

Introduction to simple (File-XI-File) scenario for starters (part 2)

https://www.sdn.sap.com/irj/sdn/weblogs?blog=/pub/wlg/1345

INSTALLATION, AUTHORIZATION, & CONNECTION ISSUES

Question 8: Business Transaction Codes

I was using 'we19' to test an inbound IDoc mbgmcr02. I got the message "status 51 qty and/or delivery completed ind or final issue ind are missing". I have the quantity filled in. I need the delivery completed "ind" or final issue "ind" filled in.

On the e1BP2017_gm_code, I use a code 02.

Can you give me the rundown on the valid codes to use here and what they mean?

A: Here is a list of Business Transactions/Events codes.

- GM_Code 01: Goods receipt for purchase order
- GM_Code 02: Goods receipt for production order
- GM_Code 03: Goods issue
- GM_Code 04: Transfer posting
- GM_Code 05: Other goods receipts
- GM_Code 06: Reversal of goods movements
- GM_Code 07: Subsequent adjustment to a subcontract order

For more details and examples, visit this link:

http://ifr.sap.com/catalog/query.asp?namespace=urn:sap-com:ifr:LO:470X200&type=bapi&name=GoodsMovement.CreateFromData

Question 9: Problems while deploying Java Proxy

We generated Java proxy of our interface and tried to deploy the same into our WAS 6.4 using NetWeaver Dev Studio.

We successfully created ".ear" file. But while deploying the file, it gave the following error:

***********************Erro r***********************
Cannot determine sdm host (is empty). Please configure your engine/sdm correctly!

***********************End**********************

The J2EE engine of XI server is configured with NWDS. Also according to the documentation of SAP, we manually restarted the SDM using 'startserver.bat' but still the problem persists.

Can you help us solve this problem?

A: Yes. Make sure that you have given message to the server port (3600) and not to the J2EE port (50000).

Instead of NWDS use SDM directly and deploy the ".ear". The ".ear" file will be there in your workspace folder when you need to use it. In your XI server, search for "RemoteGui.bat", then double click on it click on deployment, then choose your ".ear", then deploy.

Question 10: 'functiontemplate' from repository was <null>

We have a simple R/3 (RFC) to XI to R/3 (RFC) scenario that is currently working. After some time we decided to add another RFC, so we made the necessary work in IR and ID under the existing namespace and scenario respectively. We created the RFCs in every backend doing just the same steps that we did for the existing RFCs that are currently working.

When we sent the message using the new RFCs in SXMB_MONI, we encountered the error:

com.sap.aii.af.ra.ms.api.DeliveryException: error while processing message to remote system:com.sap.aii.af.rfc.core.client.RfcClientException: functiontemplate from repository was <null>

We tried to send the payload in the RWB and comparing the new RFC with the one that is working in SXMB_MONI. The difference is that the new RFC shows no response. It just appears in the payload of the receiver but no acknowledgment is shown. On the contrary, the RFC that is working shows acknowledgment:

"Legacy system to which acknowledgment message is to be sent is missing in hoplist (with wasread=false)";

So far, this is the only difference that we have noticed. We have checked the Interface Mappings and Message Mappings and everything looks like the RFCs that work.

We have shutdown java and repeated the steps re-importing the RFCs even with other names, and the error is the same.

Can you help us solve this?

A: Yes. You need to only check your RFC Communication Channel. Make sure it is working correctly.

Question 11: ExchangeProfile Problem

I installed NW04 (ABAP+J2EE) and XI. On page 33 of XI post installation, I created a user XISUPER in ABAP system and rebooted J2EE Server.

I did not find the XISUPER in the J2EE instance. Did I do something wrong here or is there any additional steps needed to be done apart from what document says? As a result, I was not able to do an import of ExchangeProfile. I search Google and SDN and found that I could use J2EE_ADMIN, but when I tried that I got the error "You are not authorized to view the requested resource".

My J2ee_admin has Administrator role and for group I have Authenticated Users, Everyone, SAP_J2EE_ADMIN.

Can you give any solution/s to this problem?

A: Two things are important for J2EE users in regards to XI.

1. During installation of J2EE you should select the XI UME option; otherwise users are stored separately in ABAP and J2EE.
2. The UME client must be the correct one as described on page 16 in the XI Install guide.

Reinstall the java system. At the point where it asks for production client, the value should match with the client which you want to use as an Integration server. 000 is the original value; you should match it with the client's. For example, if you called the client 100, then production client should also be 100. Any mismatch will result into the problem you are facing.

Question 12: XI Installation Problems

Our XI installation failed during the phase deploying SAPXIAF04_1.SCA. The displayed e rror message in SDM:

Jul 14, 2006 12:35:07... Error: Aborted: development component 'com.sap.aii.adapter.jms.app'/'sap.com'/'SAP AG'/'7.0004.20050713150837.0000':
Caught exception while checking the login credentials for SAP J2EE Engine. Check whether the SAP J2EE Engine is up and running.
com.sap.engine.deploy.manager.DeployManagerException: ERROR: Cannot connect to Host: [cixid] with user name: [J2EE_ADMIN]
Check your login information.
Exception is:
com.sap.engine.services.jndi.persistent.exceptions.NamingException: Exception while trying to get InitialContext. [Root exception is com.sap.engine.services.security.exceptions.BaseLoginException: Cannot create new RemoteLoginContext instance.]
(message ID:
com.sap.sdm.serverext.servertype.inqmy.extern.EngineApplOnlineDeployerImpl.checkLoginCredentials.DMEXC)

I have checked the login name and password is ok. There is an OSS note 756084 section 4 suggesting the problem was due to TicketLoginModule. I don't think we have changed any login modules as it is an installation. We also couldn't start the VA.

Do you have any suggestion or solution for this problem?

A: You can solve the problem by doing the following:

Configtool -> dispatcher -> Service -> P4.

For 'bindhost' option, you will need to enter your CI instance hostname/ipaddress (default is 0.0.0.0).

Question 13: XI Install Error

I was attempting to install XI on a MSCS cluster Environment - Windows Server 2003 Enterprise Edition, running Oracle 9.2.0.6. I have installed our Dev, QA and Production systems successfully. I also installed Oracle, OraFS, ABAP+Java on MSCS Cluster, and was trying to install XI Component.

When SAP installer was running, I got the following error message after I have entered the Domain, userid and password:

INFO 2006-03-08 15:46:29
Installation start: Wednesday, 08 March 2006, 15:46:25; installation directory: C:\sapinstall\XI; product to be installed: SAP NetWeaver '04 Support Release 1> NetWeaver Components Running on Java> XI Components>
Exchange Infrastructure Installation

WARNING 2006-03-08 15:46:46
The step storeSidadmPassword with step key
ExchangeInfrastructure|ind|ind|ind|ind|ind|0|Gener
icAskJavahomeAndPasswords|ind|ind|ind|ind|ind|0|st
oreSidadmPassword was executed with status
ERROR.

WARNING 2006-03-08 15:46:52
An error occurred during the installation.

The password for <SID>adm has the "@" sign in, and I wonder if this caused the error.

Is there a solution for this?

A: Yes. You need to do the following.

In the control.xml, change the line:
WindowsDomain = gui.getInputValue("fld_WindowsDomain");
To
WindowsDomain = context .get("WindowsDomain");
Continue installation.

Question 14: FTP Connection Error

I tried to run the File to IDoc scenario. In this case I used FTP as sender channel. During execution in the adapter monitor I got the following error:

Sender Adapter v1028 for Party '', Service 'FILE_BS':
Configured at 12:45:07 2006-07-06
Processing Error: Error connecting to ftp server '192.168.13.9':
com.sap.aii.adapter.file.ftp.FTPEx: /Inetpub/ftproot: The system cannot find the path specified.
last retry interval started 12:45:07 2006-07-06
length 60,000 secs

Can you tell me what caused the error?

I did all configuration everywhere and I have given everyone permission. I kept the directory in a shared folder. I am able to access the directory from XI server.

Can you tell if any other configuration is missing?

Folder path : /Inetpub/ftproot
file name : xiinput.txt

A: You need to first do a cross check on the path >> Folder path : /Inetpub/ftproot

Then check if you have assigned read/write rights to the FTP folder.

Note that if your ftproot is the FTP folder, then / is your root folder in XI adapter so if you have a folder input in ftproot, in your CC you will specify :

folder : /input

And not:

ftproot/input

Question 15: XI Lost Connection to J2EE

Sometimes, the XI system seems to lose connection to the J2EE server, and the RFC connections AI_DIRECTORY_JCOSERVER, AI_RUNTIME_JCOSERVER, etc. stops working, and then all messages fail.

Logs in dev_jcontrol show errors like:

[Thr 3596] Thu Sep 15 18:34:24 2005
[Thr 3596] ***LOG Q0I=> NiPRead: recv (10054: WSAECONNRESET: Connection reset by peer) [ninti.c 785]
[Thr 3596] *** ERROR => MsINiRead: NiBufReceive failed (NIECONN_BROKEN) [msxxi.c 2488]
[Thr 3596] *** ERROR => MsIReadFromHdl: NiRead (rc=NIECONN_BROKEN) [msxxi.c 1652]
[Thr 3596] ***LOG Q0I=> NiPConnect2: SiPeekPendConn (10065: WSAEHOSTUNREACH: No route to host) [nixxi_r.cpp 8605]
[Thr 3596] *** ERROR => MsIAttachEx: NiBufConnect to sapserver4/3601 failed (rc=NIECONN_REFUSED) [msxxi.c 633]
[Thr 3596] *** WARNING => Can't reconnect to message server (sapserver4/3601) [rc = -100]-> reconnect [jcntrms.c 296]
[Thr 6612] ***LOG Q0I=> NiPRead: recv (10054: WSAECONNRESET: Connection reset by peer) [ninti.c 785]

[Thr 3596] Thu Sep 15 18:34:29 2005
[Thr 3596] *** ERROR => MsIAttachEx: NiBufConnect to sapserver4/3601 failed (rc=NIECONN_REFUSED) [msxxi.c 633]
[Thr 3596] *** WARNING => Can't reconnect to message server (sapserver4/3601) [rc = -100]-> reconnect [jcntrms.c 296]

Do you have any suggestions concerning this problem?

A: I see this issue often in our XI systems. To date, there is only one solution: restart the JCos. We have not been able to determine why these JCos lose their registration in the gateway, but they do.

The next time it happens, go to tcode SMGW and go to "Logged on clients". You should see the above mentioned RFC's logged onto the gateway. If you don't then open the VA on the XI server to stop then start each affected JCo. Once it is restarted, check the gateway again to see if they have registered. Your system will be good to go without restarting the entire J2EE engine.

Question 16: JCo Connection Parameters and Migration through Dev/QA/Prod

I know how to open up from within XI a JCo connection to an SAP client.

How do you determine what SAP client to connect to and how to migrate that along when you move the XI development from Dev to QA to Prod?

A: You will need to manage with a "prop file". Just give it the same name on the three systems (Dev, QA, and Production). Keep it in a separate 'Imported Archive' (separate java package as well), and load it from java as resource. You can do this in 1 SWCV and then have others base themselves off of that one so you only have to do it once.

If you cannot upload objects directly into QA and Production, a "prop file" on the "filesystem" is better. Choose a suitable location existing on the three systems.

When using the Lookup API with RFC/JCo, you still need the name of the "Service without Pary". Y ou have to put this name in a properties file on the "filesystem" of the XI server. The file will have the same name (but different contents) on Dev, QA and Production.

You can also use the SAP XI value mapping to store configuratio n parameters in.

Question 17: sm58 - Name or Password is Incorrect

I have encountered a problem. After the configuration of an IDoc to File, I am facing an error "sm58" after successfully sending an IDoc with "we19".

Status text indicated: "Name or password is incorrect. Please re-enter".

After retrying, I've got a new error message:

"User is locked. Please notify the person responsible".

How do I sort this out?

A: You need to check your SM59 connection (Target system column in SM58). There is most probably a userid/password defined that is incorrect. You have to unlock the user in the target system.

Be careful. Normally, when you try to access your SAP systems with an invalid user id / password more than 3 times, the user gets locked. You will have to ask your admin to unlock the user and then make your remote log on test in Sm 59.

Cross check first with these steps in what you have done so far.

While doing an IDoc to XI to File scenario, the points to take note of are as follows:

1. You don't need a DT, MT or a message interface for the IDoc as it itself acts as the Message Interface.
2. You import the IDoc and use the same in your mapping.
3. In this configuration, note that you don't have a sender agreement as you don't have a sender IDoc adapter.

If it is that you wanted to send an IDoc from XI (File to IDoc), then in this case:

Points 1 and 2 will remain, but the 3rd will not. You will need a sender agreement for the file and a receiver agreement for the IDoc.

IDoc to File scenario reference:

https://www.sdn.sap.com/irj/sdn/weblogs?blog=/pub/wlg/1819

Configurations in R/3 side:

1. SM 59 (RFC destinations)

   Create a RFC destination on the XI server. The connection type should be R/3 connection. The target host needs to be the XI server.

2. WE 21 (Ports in IDoc processing)

   Create a transactional port. Provide the RFC destination created in this.

3. BD 54

   Create a logical system.

4. WE 20 (Partner Profiles)

   a. Create a new partner profile under partner type LS.

   b. Assign the message type in outbound parameters.

   c. Open the message type (Dbl click) and configure the receiver port to the port created.

XI Server Configurations:

1. SM59 (RFC destination)

   Configure the RFC destination specific to the R/3 system.

2. IDX1 (Port maintenance in IDoc Adapter)

Create a port and provide the RFC destination.

TESTING:

WE19 for pushing the IDoc in XI through trfc port.

To be able to trigger your IDOC from the SAP ISU system, you will have to set the partner profile in "we20". Select your Business System (mostly under Logical system) and then create outbound entries for whichever IDoc you want to trigger.

You define your basic type also in your partner profile settings. Please go thru the following links to get a better idea about partner profile:

http://help.sap.com/saphelp_nw04/helpdata/en/dc/6b833243d711d1893e0000e8323c4f/frameset.htm

http://help.sap.com/saphelp_nw04/helpdata/en/dc/6b7cd343d711d1893e0000e8323c4f/frameset.htm

http://help.sap.com/saphelp_nw04/helpdata/en/32/692037b1f10709e10000009b38f839/content.htm

http://help.sap.com/saphelp_nw04/helpdata/en/5e/b8f8bf356dc84096e4fedc2cd71426/frameset.htm

I would suggest that you go through these blogs if any more issue arises.

https://weblogs.sdn.sap.com/pub/wlg/1439

https://weblogs.sdn.sap.com/pub/wlg/1843

Question 18: "You are not authorized to view the requested resource in SLD"

After logging into SXMB_IFR, I tried to get some SLD components but I instead got the "You are not authorized to view the requested resource in SLD".

What do I need to do to get into SLD?

A: You will need to check the role or level of authorization you have.

SAP_SLD_ADMINISTRATOR

Or

SAP_SLD_CONFIGURATOR

Or

SAP_XI_CONFIGURATOR

Or

SAP_XI_CONTENT_ORGANIZER

For a complete definition of roles and level of authorization, check out the following link.

http://help.sap.com/saphelp_nw04/helpdata/en/c4/51104159ecef23e10000000a155106/content.htm

Question 19: RWB Error during Message Monitoring

I got the following error during Message monitoring:

"User XIRWBUSER has no RFC authorization for function group HTTPTREE, error key: RFC_ERROR_SYSTEM_FAILURE"

What can this mean and how do I fix it?

A: First, check if your XIRWBUSER has its standard roles.

SAP_XI_RWB_SERV_USER
SAP_XI_RWB_SERV_USER_MAIN

Normally the mentioned roles should be sufficient.

Another key is the SP level of your XI system. After a new SP level, XI will request more authorizations which have not been included in the standard role so far. You will need to open up an OSS message at SAP.

The standard role has been extended with a new SP but the according profile has not been regenerated, so you will also need to carry out a mass generation of all profiles for SAP_XI roles and after that a user comparison.

Question 20: Websphere MQ Problem

I have a problem with Websphere MQ Sender adapter. I know that in the queue are messages but XI doesn't get them. I have checked everything in the adapter engine and integration engine.

There are no errors and all lights are green. There is no payload.

How do I make the adapter work?

A: Yes. You need to reset your communication channel. Deactivate and activate it again.

Question 21: Reassigning Change List to a Different User

One user in our system has changed SWCV, but did not activate the change list. The system pops out the message saying:

"If necessary, you can reassign the other user's change list to yourself"

How do I find what the system requires?

A: Open the Integration Builder Web Start application and go to the "change list" tab. Select the user that has changed the SWCV and press "Display". You can now assign the change list to yours if you right-click on it and press "OK".

Question 22: Setting up HTTPS

We added an SSL certificate to our XI server. We are struggling our way through the documentation for the steps to exchange messages via HTTPS.

How do I set the adapter to use HTTPS in the integration directory?

I only see HTTP 1.0 in the options for protocol while trying to setup the HTTP adapter settings.

The external party is the receiver of messages from us. During testing, no security was in place so we tried sending to a URL using the HTTP adapter. Now, HTTPS protocol must be used. However, for the HTTP adapter type, HTTPS protocol is not a drop down option.

Does that mean I have to use adapter type "XI" to send to a URL via HTTPS?

A: You need to do the following to fix your problem.

In the communication channel select the following:

- Transport protocol : HTTP1.0
- Addressing Type : HTTP Destination
- HTTP Destination: your ABAP RFC (type G)

In your RFC destination, you need to specify the URL and the certificate to use to connect to your server.

ADAPTER & ADAPTER ENGINE FAQ

Question 23: Adapter Engine

I need to change the host name of the adapter engine that is showing up in RWB under integration server.

How do I accomplish this?

A: The host name displayed in RWB is nothing but XI server's host name. If you change server host name, it will reflect there.

Visit the following link for more details:

http://help.sap.com/saphelp_nw04/helpdata/en/ea/f02840d89d185de10000000a1550b0/frameset.htm

Question 24: Adapter Engine not found in ID

I just installed my system with XI3.0 SP12 and this adapter engine problem occurred while developing my first integration scenario , IDoc - File.

Adapter Engine for File adapter in not available to select from drop down while configuring CC.

An SLDCHECK gave this result:

'no corresponding biz system found for xi system' ==> check and maintain the SLD content for the current system

EXCHANGE_PROFILE_GET_PARAMETER function:
returned exception code 2
Access to the XI profile is currently disrupted'

What could have caused this problem? Can you help me solve this?

A: Given that this is a new installation,check that the XI Content for SAP Basis 6.40 (SP12 since that's what your XI system is on) has been imported into the 'Integration Repository'. This is one of the post-installation steps defined in the Install Guide. Within this is the adapter metadata for all the delivered adapters. Without this, you'll have this problem and others.

Also, check that you have adequately carried out all the post-installation steps of the install guide. It is critical that this be done before moving on to design and configuration of scenarios.

Question 25: Adapter Engine Errors

This is a JDBC receiver scenario.

A message that fails with a 'System Error in Adapter Engine' does not raise alerts but 'Integration engine - system error' messages raises alerts.

What I mean is in message monitoring - choosing Integration Server and displaying the messages (messages with status system error and engine to adapter engine) does not raise alerts.

Can you give a clarification concerning this matter?

A: If you are on:

SP12 - There is no way for you to raise alerts.

SP13 - You can configure CCMS to raise alerts for Adapter Engine.

SP14 on wards - You have the option of specifying adapter alert rules.

Alert configuration may sometimes cause some problems. With the steps provided in the link below you can quickly find out what might be the reason.

https://www.sdn.sap.com/irj/sdn/weblogs?blog=/pub/wlg/2327

http://help.sap.com/saphelp_nw04/helpdata/en/80/942f3ffed33d67e10000000a114084/frameset.htm

http://help.sap.com/saphelp_nw04/helpdata/en/c4/3a60e3505211d189550000e829fbbd/frameset.htm

The link below gives you a better idea of alert management.

https://www.sdn.sap.com/irj/sdn/weblogs?blog=/pub/wlg/1165

Question 26: J2SE Adapter Engine / JMS Adapter

We need to connect to MQ Series 5.3 (Websphere MQ) from the XI (3.0 SP16) box.

Do J2SE adapter engine need to be enabled/configured in order to use JMS Adapter? Can't we use J2EE JMSAdapter instead of J2SE JMS Adapter? Where can I download the JMS Adapter libraries, for installation?

Ours is UNIX-based installation.

I have gone thru the thread below and the SAP Note: 747601 that talks about J2EE JMSAdapter MQSeries libraries.

https://www.sdn.sap.com/irj/sdn/thread?forumID=44&threadID=136959&messageID=1532727

A: Standard JMS adapter comes with XI. When you are trying to connect to external systems like "MQ" or "Sonic", you need to get the "client" files from the vendor and then you need to deploy the same in your XI.

The following link will give you the step by step procedure.

https://www.sdn.sap.com/irj/servlet/prt/portal/prtroot/docs/library/uuid/3867a582-0401-0010-6cbf-9644e49f1a10

You can download the libraries from the market place. Also go through the following link on how to deploy them.

https://www.sdn.sap.com/irj/servlet/prt/portal/prtroot/docs/library/uuid/3867a582-0401-0010-6cbf-9644e49f1a10

Finally, these following links are good for future references.

https://www.sdn.sap.com/irj/sdn/thread?threadID=138621

https://www.sdn.sap.com/irj/sdn/thread?threadID=67676

http://help.sap.com/saphelp_nw04/helpdata/en/6f/246b3de666930fe10000000a114084/frameset.htm

https://www.sdn.sap.com/irj/servlet/prt/portal/prtroot/docs/library/uuid/03fd85cc-0201-0010-8ca4-a32a119a582d

https://www.sdn.sap.com/irj/sdn/thread?threadID=55291

https://www.sdn.sap.com/irj/sdn/thread?threadID=136959

Question 27: Ping Error in RWB for J2SE Adapter Engine

We have several external J2SE adapter engines and they function great other than from a monitoring perspective. In RWB "Ping Status", I'm getting the following:

HTTP request failed. Error code: "401". Error message: "Authorization Required"

Do you have any idea what's causing this?

A: You will need to check the following:

1. If user: XIRWBUSER is not locked in R/3
2. If you got a correct password in the XI exchange profile:
    a. com.sap.aii.rwb.serviceuser.name
    b. com.sap.aii.rwb.serviceuser.pwd
    c. com.sap.aii.rwb.serviceuser.language

Question 28: RFC Adapter Problem: Adapter Engine Field Blank

I want to invoke a BAPI defined on an R/3 system. I am trying to create a RFC Adapter in the Integration Directory by creating a communication channel.

The problem I am facing is that when I define the Adapter Type as RFC, the Adapter Engine dropdown list is blank and it does not contain any entries.

On passing a document through XI, I can see the following error in the monitor:

<SAP:Code
area="INTERNAL">ADAPTER_NAME_INVALID</SAP:Code>
<SAP:P1>RFC</SAP:P1>
<SAP:P2>PLSRV_CALL_ADAPTER</SAP:P2>
<SAP:P3 />
<SAP:P4 />
<SAP:AdditionalText />
<SAP:ApplicationFaultMessage namespace="" />
<SAP:Stack>Unknown receiver adapter (name = RFC)</SAP:Stack>

What do I need to configure on the XI and R/3 side?

The following entries appear in the SLD for content maintenance, class XI Integration Server. My machine name is netweaver and SID is NW4.

XI Contained Integration Server
GroupComponent: XI Domain Domain netweaver
XI Integration Server Logical Identity
SameElement: Business System NW4

A: Your problem is caused by a mess-up in SLD when the installation was done. Your SLD is missing a third entry:

"XI Sub-System viewed application system";

After you add this, you need to restart the SLD server from SLD administration page.

If you are still not getting the populated adapter engine list, you will need to configure your business and technical systems correctly, make the necessary associations, and then you will be able to see the Integration Server in the RFC adapter drop down.

Question 29: Error in Adapter Engine

We installed XI 3.0 SP9 with jre 1.4.2-08. When I selected the 'Adapter type' as File in 'Sender' mode while configuring the scenario FILE-IDoc by following the weblog in the Integration directory, I did not get the values for Adapter Engine (Integration Server), which is mandatory. But when I selected IDoc, XI adapter types, I was able to get Integration Server.

I checked in the Runtime workbench, Adapter Monitoring, and there I saw an error in SLD access saying that JPR configuration is not done. I concluded that the problem is with the configuration of Adapter Engine.

How can I solve this problem?

A: You need to create a business system BS_JPR for Web AS Java type. You will see the JPR turning green. This is not related to the integration directory in your case.

The default adapter engine is Integration Server. There couldbe more if you have installed PCK or another XI instance.

You will have to use the Integration Server Adapter Engine.

You will also need to restart your XI server after the above steps.

Question 30: Decentralized Adapter Engine

We have installed an XI landscape (XID, XIQ, and XIP) on UNIX along with a single decentralized Adapter Engine on Windows (XD1) which is currently configured for use with our XID system. We would like to also use this same decentralized Adapter Engine with our XIQ system. However, when we export a communication channel from XID (configured to use the decentralized adapter engine af.XID.calxid1 and subsequently import the communication channel into XIQ), the decentralized Adapter engine that was configured in XID (af.XD1.calxid1) was replaced with "I ntegration Server" (Default) in the Communication Channel configuration in XIQ. The pull down to choose an adapter engine shows only the (Default) Integration server as an available choice. Currently XID and XIQ are using the same SLD and the decentralized adapter engine (af.XD1.calxid1) is identified there. I have been unable to determine how to use the decentralized adapter engine with our XIQ system.

Does anyone know whether it is possible to have multiple XI systems using the same de-centralized Adapter Engine? And if it is possible, how do you configure the second XI system (XIQ) to use the decentralized adapter engine?

A: No, it is not possible to have multiple XI systems use the same decentralized Adapter Engine. A decentralized Adapter Engine can only be attached to a single Integration Server. Best solution is to install another decentralized Adapter Engine for every XI system.

Question 31: Unable to Find any Adapter Engines

I tried to execute a scenario. An xml-file is read from a drive by the XI system. XI read the values. Another xml-file containing some parts of this info was written to another location. I saw that the file was read and removed.

However, when I checked the monitoring, I found following error message:


```
<SAP:Error xmlns:SAP="http://sap.com/xi/XI/Message/30"
xmlns:SOAP="http://schemas.xmlsoap.org/soap/envelope/"
SOAP:mustUnderstand="">
<SAP:Category>XIServer</SAP:Category>
<SAP:Code
area="INTERNAL">AE_DETAILS_GET_ERROR</SAP:Code>
<SAP:P1>af.cx1.cernum05\cx1</SAP:P1>
<SAP:P2 />
<SAP:P3 />
<SAP:P4 />
<SAP:AdditionalText>Exception in SLD client:
AbapSLDRequestHandler.exe: Unable to find any Adapter
Engines</SAP:AdditionalText>
<SAP:ApplicationFaultMessage namespace="" />
<SAP:Stack>Error when reading the access data (URL, user, password)
for the Adapter Engine af.cx1.cernum05\cx1</SAP:Stack>
<SAP:Retry>M</SAP:Retry>
</SAP:Error>
```


Is there some configuration missing? Are there things which I missed to check out?

We are running XI3.0 SP9.

A: You need to execute transaction SE37 and test the function module SAI_AE_DETAILS_GET. Enter your AE_NAME af.<hostname>.<sysid> and execute.

You also need to run an SLDCHECK and check whether your exchange profile parameter checks are successful. The last one Calling function EXCHANGE_PROFILE_GET_PARAMETER.

If these are correct, check that your com.sap.aii.adapterframework.serviceuser.name and com.sap.aii.adapterframework.serviceuser.pwd are correct.

If these are correct, check whether the user id is locked.

Also check whether you are using the SLD which is on your XI server or you are p ointing to a different SLD.

Question 32: File Adapter Command

I am running a command after a message processing is complete. If the UNIX command fails, is there a way to have that show up as a failure in SXMB_MONI?

A: You will not see any status in SXMB_MONI, since the message has been sent successfully to the file adapter.

However, in RWB, for adapter message monitoring, there will be a warning indicating the command has failed.

If you want to debug because you can not see any status in SXMB_MONI, visit:

https://www.sdn.sap.com/irj/sdn/weblogs?blog=/pub/wlg/2184

Question 33: Receiver Mail Adapter

I tried to configure an HTTP to XI to mail adapter. I used my company's mail address for this. I don't get any errors in SXMB_MONI and RWB, but the mail is not delivered to my inbox. I checked the Message monitoring.

The detailed audit log shows:

2006-08-29 14:46:23 Success output 1156842983828 The message was successfully received by the messaging system. Profile: XI URL: http://sap1:50000/MessagingSystem/receive/AFW/XI
2006-08-29 14:46:23 Success output 1156842983843 Using connection AFW. Trying to put the message into the receive queue.
2006-08-29 14:46:23 Success SAPEngine_Application_Thread[impl:3]_11 1156842983875 The message was successfully retrieved from the receive queue.
2006-08-29 14:46:23 Success SAPEngine_Application_Thread[impl:3]_11 1156842983937 The message status set to DLNG.
2006-08-29 14:46:23 Success SAPEngine_Application_Thread[impl:3]_11 1156842983968 Delivering to channel: CC_MailTest
2006-08-29 14:46:24 Success SAPEngine_Application_Thread[impl:3]_11 1156842984000 Mail: message entering the adapter
2006-08-29 14:46:44 Error SAPEngine_Application_Thread[impl:3]_11 1156843004953 Exception caught by adapter framework: Failed to call the endpoint
2006-08-29 14:46:44 Error SAPEngine_Application_Thread[impl:3]_11 1156843004953 Delivery of the message to the application using connection AFW failed, due to: Failed to call the endpoint.
2006-08-29 14:46:44 Success SAPEngine_Application_Thread[impl:3]_11 1156843004984 The asynchronous message was successfully scheduled to be delivered at Tue Aug 29 14:51:44 GMT+05:30 2006.
2006-08-29 14:46:45 Success SAPEngine_Application_Thread[impl:3]_11 1156843005000 The message status set to WAIT.

The parameters of the mail adapter are:

Transport Protocol : SMTP
Message Protocol : XIALL
Adapter Engine : Integration Server

url : smtp://<server name>.caritor.com
user : jaishankar
password : ******

From : jaishankar.ramakrishnan@caritor.com
To : jaishankar.ra makrishnan@caritor.com
Subject : test mail from XI

I think these parameters are correct.

Why can't the mail get delivered to my inbox?

A: Yes, your parameters seem to be correct. The only thing you can do is to ask your "basis people" if your XI server has access to the company mail server (opened ports, etc.) Also check with your office email admin team whether the SMTP address entered is correct or not.

Question 34: Adapter Monitor Message

In a file to file to scenario, I got the following message in Adapter monitor:

"Receiver Adapter v1027 for Party '', Service 'YAMAHA_BS':
Configured at 18:31:43 2008-10-17
Up and running - no message processing until now"

What exactly is this error?

A: This is not an error message.

"Up and running - no message processing until now";

Your receiver file adapter is ready to poll the data as it has been configured successfully. It means that XI receiver adapter has not processed any messages until now. If the sender has picked the file, check it in SXMB_MONI; there might be some error.

Question 35: Setting the Username & Password for the Plain HTTP Adapter

When I passed in a HTTP request into the integration engine's plain_http adapter url, I was required to give a username and a password for authentication.

Is it possible to set this username and password globally somewhere?

This is to avoid the username and password to be given again and again for each message. The requirement is like all http messages from our partners will be routed through a proxy in the DMZ which would have an authentication and we do not want the XI user credentials to be given again repeatedly.

A: You need to use SICF, then sap/xi/adapter_plain, then change button. Enter client, username, password, and language.

If you want to just test the http adapter use this code:

```
<html>

<script type="text/javascript">;
<!--
function button1_onclick() {
var result = "Result: ";
var payload = "<?xml version=\"1.0\" encoding=\"UTF-8\" ?>";
// escape "http://"
var senderNamespace =
escape(document.MessageParameters.SenderNamespace.value);

var reqString = "http://"
reqString = reqString +
document.MessageParameters.Server.value+":";
reqString = reqString + document.MessageParameters.Port.value +
"/sap/xi/adapter_plain?";
reqString = reqString + "namespace=" + senderNamespace;
reqString = reqString + "&interface=" +
document.MessageParameters.SenderInterface.value;
reqString = reqString + "&service=" +
document.MessageParameters.SenderService.value;
```

```
reqString = reqString + "&party=" +
document.MessageParameters.SenderParty.value;
reqString = reqString + "&agency=" +
document.MessageParameters.SenderAgency.value;
reqString = reqString + "&scheme=" +
document.MessageParameters.SenderScheme.value;
reqString = reqString + "&QOS=" +
document.MessageParameters.qos.value;

reqString = reqString + "&queueid=httpclient";

reqString = reqString + "&sap-user=" +
document.MessageParameters.username.value;
reqString = reqString + "&sap-password=" +
document.MessageParameters.password.value;
reqString = reqString + "&sap-client=" +
document.MessageParameters.Client.value
reqString = reqString + "&sap-language=EN";
var xhttp = new ActiveXObject("msxml2.xmlhttp");

for (var i=0; i<document.MessageParameters.retry.value; i++) {

  xhttp.open ("POST", reqString, false);
 document.MessageParameters.URL.value=reqString;

  if (document.MessageParameters.Source[0].checked == true) {
   payload = "<?xml version=\"1.0\" encoding=\"UTF-8\" ?> "+
document.MessageParameters.xmlData.value;
   xhttp.send (payload);
  } else{
   var xmlDoc = new ActiveXObject("microsoft.xmldom");
   xmlDoc.async=false;
   xmlDoc.load (document.MessageParameters.xmlFile.value);
   xhttp.send (xmlDoc);
  }
result = result + "\nhttp-Status:  " + xhttp.status + " " + xhttp.statusText
+ " \nPayload:\n" + xhttp.responseText;

xhttp.close;
document.MessageParameters.response.value=result;
}

}
```

```
//-->
</script>
<head></head>

<body>

<h3>Client Http Adapter </h3>
<form name="MessageParameters">
<table border="1" cellpadding="0" cellspacing="0" style="border-
collapse: collapse" bordercolor="#111111" width="100%">
<h4>Header</h4>
<tbody>
<tr>
<td width="10%"><label>Server Host</label> </td>
<td width="22%">

<!-- Change server and port here -->

<input type="text" id="host" name="Server"
value="YourServer" size="20" /> </td>
<td width="10%"><label>Server Port</label> </td>
<td width="22%"><input type="text" id="port" name="Port"
value="8000" size="10" /> </td>
</tr>
<tr>
<td width="10%">Client</td>
<td width="22%">

<!-- Change client here -->

<input type="text" id="client" name="Client"
value="100" size="3" /></td>
<td width="10%"> </td>
<td width="22%"> </td>
</tr>
<tr>
<td width="10%"><label>Sender Service</label> </td>
<td width="22%">

<!-- Change sender service here -->

<input type="text" id="senderService"
name="SenderService" value="TravelAgencyCS" size="40" /> </td>
```

```
<td width="10%">Quality of Service</td>
<td width="22%">
    <select size="1" name="qos">
    <option value="BE">Best Effort (synchronous)</option>
    <option value="EO" selected>Exactly Once
(asynchronous)</option>
    <option value="EOIO">Exactly Once in Order</option>
    </select>
</td>
</tr>
<tr>
<td width="10%"><label>Sender Interface</label> </td>

<!-- Change sender interface name here -->

<td width="22%"><input type="text" id="senderInterface"
name="SenderInterface" value="BookingOrdersOut" size="40" />
</td>
<td width="10%"><label>Sender Namespace</label> </td>
<td width="22%">

<!-- Change sender interface namespace  here -->

<input type="text" id="senderNamespace"
name="SenderNamespace"
value="http://sap.com/xi/rkt/CaseStudy/group99"
size="40" /></td>
</tr>
</tbody>
</table>
<br>
<table border="1" cellpadding="0" cellspacing="0" style="border-
collapse: collapse" bordercolor="#111111" width="100%">
<h4>Optional Parameters</h4>
<tbody>
<tr>
<td width="10%">Sender Party</td>
<td width="22%"><input type="text" id="senderParty"
name="SenderParty" size="40" /></td>
</tr>
<tr>
<td width="10%">Sender Agency</td>
<td width="22%"><input type="text" id="senderAgency"
```

```
name="SenderAgency" size="40" /></td>
<td width="10%">Sender Scheme</td>
<td width="22%"><input type="text" id="senderScheme"
name="SenderScheme" size="40" /></td>
</tr>

 <TR>
   <TD width="10%">Username</TD>

<!-- Change user name here -->

    <TD width="22%"><INPUT id=username size=40 value=xiappluser
name=username></TD>
    <TD width="10%">Password</TD>
    <TD width="22%"><INPUT id=password type=password size=40
name=password></TD></TR>
  <TR>
    <TD width="10%">Retry</TD>
    <TD width="22%"><INPUT id=retry type=number size=40 value=1
name=retry></TD>
 </TR>

</tbody>
</table>
<br>
<table border="1" cellpadding="0" cellspacing="0" style="border-
collapse: collapse" bordercolor="#111111" width="100%">
<h4>Payload</h4>
<tbody>
<tr>
<fieldset style="padding: 2">
<td width="50%"><input type="radio" name="Source"
value="Textarea" checked="checked" />Type in XML</td>
<td width="50%"><input type="radio" name="Source" value="File"
/>Upload File</td>
</fieldset>
</tr>
<tr>
<td width="50%"><textarea name="xmlData" rows="10"
cols="60">&lt;a&gt;test&lt;/a&gt;</textarea></td>
<td width="50%"><input type="file" name="xmlFile" size="40" />
</td>
</tr>
```

```
</tbody>
</table>
<p>
<input type="button" value="Send" id="button1" name="button1"
LANGUAGE="javascript" onclick="button1_onclick()" />
</p>
<hr />
<table border="1" cellpadding="0" cellspacing="0" style="border-
collapse: collapse" bordercolor="#111111" width="100%">
<h4>Result</h4>
  <P align=left>URL: <TEXTAREA name=URL
cols=104></TEXTAREA></P>
  <P align=left> </P>
<tbody>
<tr>
<td width="50%"><textarea name="response" rows="5"
cols="60"></textarea></td>
</tr>
</tbody>
</table>
</form>

</body>

</html>
```

The code is now updated to allow multiple messages and for new input fields for User and Password.

This HTML code was originally introduced by Joachim Orb for educational purposes.

You can find a description here:

https://www.sdn.sap.com/irj/servlet/prt/portal/prtroot/docs/library/uuid/66dadc6e-0a01-0010-9ea9-bb6d8ca48cc8

I recommend that you overwrite the required parameters direct in the HTML source.

Question 36: File adapter Wildcard

Is it possible to read files with different names with one (1) file adapter communication channel?

Ex: I want to read all the files that start with "abc".

A: Yes, it is possible.

This is an example of how you do it.

abc*

Take note that it is case sensitive.

For additional details, visit:

http://help.sap.com/saphelp_nw04/helpdata/en/e3/94007075cae04f930cc4c034e411e1/content.htm

Question 37: Sync Receiver JDBC Adapter

I tried to make a synchronous call to a receiver JDBC adapter with the help of:

https://www.sdn.sap.com/irj/sdn/weblogs?blog=/pub/wlg/3928.

I got the following error in the JDBC adapter:

com.sap.aii.af.ra.ms.api.DeliveryException: ERROR:Processing request: Error when executing statement for table/stored proc. 'MISDetails': java.sql.SQLException: FATAL ERROR document format: structure 'STATEMENT', key element 'FiscalYear' contains no values

My Source message is:

```
<?xml version="1.0" encoding="UTF-8"?>
<ns:MT_FILE_OUT xmlns:ns="urn:ters">
<REQUEST>
<FISCALYEAR>2007</FISCALYEAR>
<YEARMONTH>1</YEARMONTH>
<OPERATION>EQ</OPERATION>
</REQUEST>
</ns:MT_FILE_OUT>
```

And JDBC request message is ..

```
<?xml version="1.0" encoding="UTF-8"?>
<ns:MT_JDBC_REQ xmlns:ns="urn:ters">
<STATEMENT>
<TABLENAMEACTION="SELECT">
<TABLE>MISDetails</TABLE>
</TABLENAME>
<ACCESS>
<FiscalYear> </FiscalYear>
<YearMonth> </YearMonth><ProductCode>
</ProductCode><TargetVolume> </TargetVolume>
</ACCESS>
<KEY>
<FiscalYear compareOperation="EQ">2007</FiscalYear>
</KEY>
</STATEMENT>
</ns:MT_JDBC_REQ>
```

Can you help me sort this out?

A: The problem is that </TABLENAME> was closed earlier than necessary.

This is how the JDBC data type should be:

```
<?xml version="1.0" encoding="UTF-8"?>
<ns:MT_JDBC_REQ xmlns:ns="urn:ters">
<STATEMENT>
<TABLENAME ACTION="SELECT">
<TABLE>MISDetails</TABLE>
<ACCESS>
<FiscalYear> </FiscalYear>
<YearMonth> </YearMonth>
<ProductCode> </ProductCode>
<TargetVolume> </TargetVolume>
</ACCESS>
<KEY>
<FiscalYear compareOperation="EQ">2007</FiscalYear>
</KEY>
</TABLENAME>
</STATEMENT>
</ns:MT_JDBC_REQ>
```

The TABLE, ACCESS and KEY come under the TABLENAME tag.

Question 38: Outbound File Adapter

I am trying to create an outbound file adapter, designed to receive XML messages from XI Integration engine and store it in a file.

Reading from the document "Configuring the Receiver File/FTP Adapter",

http://help.sap.com/saphelp_nw04/helpdata/en/bc/bb79d6061007419a081e58cbeaaf28/content.htm

I believe that configuration should look like this:

```
-------------------------------------
## file adapter java class
classname=com.sap.aii.messaging.adapter.ModuleXMB2FILE
version=30

mode=XMB2FILE

##Bind the address for Integration port to connect to
XI.httpPort=1981
XI.httpService=/TempFileTran

file.TargetFilename=mindichFile.txt
file.writeMode=overwrite
-------------------------------------
```

The response I receive is "version not set" and adapter does not start running.

Is there a way to correct this? I use a XI 2.0 SR1.

A: The configuration "version=30" has to be removed. It is not needed in the file adapter.

Although the documentation specifically mentions the fact that "version=30" must exists, it is version dependent.

If you use J2SE adapters to connect with XI3, you may need to put the version configuration.

Question 39: J2SE Adapter Registration

I tried using SLD Access service on J2SE adapter but it does not work. This J2SE Adapter Engine is registered in the SLD. My J2SE adapter was never available in the configuration means; in the communication channel ex: file adapter, the adapter engine drop down and all I have is Integration Server. My J2SE adapter was never listed there.

How do you register J2SE adapter with XI?

A: First, see page 10 of "SAP XI Release 3.0 SR1" installation guide.

http://help.sap.com/bp_bpmv130/Documentation/Installation/XI30InstallGuide.pdf#search=%22SAP%20XI%20SR1%20installation%20guide%22

It mentions the disadvantage of just plain J2SE adapter engine as "Less integration into the SAP XI environment due to lack of central configuration and monitoring services".

It makes sense because in SLD you can only create technical/business system as Web AS Java (say for J2EE decentralized adapter engine) and not as J2SE adapter engine.

But if you want a receiver file adapter, you need to maintain in the adapter configuration:

```
XI.httpPort=<port_no>
XI.httpService=<service>
```

Then in the communication channel, you choose XI protocol (XI 3.0) and as URL you enter:

http://<J2SE-host>:<port_no>/<service>

eg:

XI.httpPort=1234
XI.httpService=/file/Receiver

-> http://<J2SE-host>:1234/file/Receiver

The file adapter business system needs to be created in SLD to which you will send the message using XML protocol (XI Adapter). The standalone adapter in the business system will then do the XMB2File conversion.

Question 40: Problem with SOAP adapter

I have configured the SOAP adapter to send a message through to a WS-I compliant web service.

I got the following error message:

```
<?xml version="1.0" encoding="UTF-8" standalone="yes" ?>
- <!-- Call Adapter
-->
- <SAP:Error xmlns:SAP="http://sap.com/xi/XI/Message/30"
xmlns:SOAP="http://schemas.xmlsoap.org/soap/envelope/"
SOAP:mustUnderstand="1">
<SAP:Category>XIAdapter</SAP:Category>
<SAP:Code
area="PARSING">ADAPTER.SOAP_EXCEPTION</SAP:Code>
<SAP:P1 />
<SAP:P2 />
<SAP:P3 />
<SAP:P4 />
<SAP:AdditionalText>soap fault: Server did not recognize the value of
HTTP Header SOAPAction: .</SAP:AdditionalText>
<SAP:ApplicationFaultMessage namespace="" />
<SAP:Stack />
<SAP:Retry>M</SAP:Retry>
</SAP:Error>
```

Can you point me to the right direction?

A: Your server requires a SOAP-Action.

If you have a WSDL for the message, look at the attributesoapAction of the tag soap:operation. Take the parameter there and type the value in the SOAP adapter receiver channel configuration.

Question 41: RFC Adapter as Sender

We have a business scenario wherein I have to execute the RFC function (asynchronous) from an ABAP in R/3 and update the data in DB2 tables (asynchronous).

I used RFC as sender (asynchronous) and JDBC as receiver (asynchronous). I configured/registered the RFC connection in SM59 and used the same program id in RFC sender adapter. I tested the connection in standalone mode and it is working.

The RFC function, when I imported, will have a request and a response. The data that I require to send to JDBC adapter is in the response. I tried to use RFC response and created a message interface. Then I used that in my interface mapping and also in the sender & receiver agreements. In the message mapping I used, response was imported.

I got an error message “sender agreement not found”. I changed the sender agreement to use RFC function as sender interface, but I cannot use this function module for my mapping, as it does not contain the response.

I deleted the sender/receiver agreements and receiver/interface determination. Then I started creating a new interface determination but I can’t find the interface mapping as the interface mapping user response.

In my business scenario I need a user interface before calling the RFC function. I wrote a wrapper around the RFC which will provide me with user interface; then I would like to send the response data to XI using RFC sender.

We are on XI3.0 SP13. I have to use the response of the RFC in the message mapping. It should be able to send the data to JDBC Adapter.

How do I fixthis?

A: If you want to capture the response of an RFC execution in XI and then map this response to another structure (in your case a JDBC structure) inside XI message mapping, then you will have to use the RFC receiver adapter of XI and NOT the RFC sender adapter. If you use the RFC sender adapter, it means that your SAP system is acting as an RFC CLIENT. What happens is the REQUEST structure in your RFC destination will be converted to RFC-XML by the RFC sender adapter of XI and is available for further processing.

If you want to send the RESPONSE structure of an RFC to XI , one way is to execute the RFC in SAP (without passing this thru XI). Now you have to pass the result of this RFC execution to XI by assigning it to a request structure of another RFC in your ABAP code and pass it to XI using RFC sender adapter. If not , you can use a dummy RFC in SAP to send a trigger to XI, execute the actual RFC in XI using RFC receiver adapter, capture the response, map it to your JDBC structure and you are done.

Check out these threads for additional reference:

https://forums.sdn.sap.com/thread.jspa?forumID=44&threadID=39026&messageID=378929#378929

https://forums.sdn.sap.com/thread.jspa?forumID=44&threadID=57874&messageID=607693#607693

https://forums.sdn.sap.com/thread.jspa?forumID=44&threadID=33356&messageID=313604#313604

Question 42: JDBC Adapter

I have a scenario where I have to take data from a Relational Database System which is the sender and invoke a BAPI in the receiver system.

How do I get the JDBC adapter to read only entries in DB that has been newly created and not the ones that has been read earlier?

A: You need to have some sort of flag set in the DB table so that every time the Sender Adapter reads the data, it updates the flag accordingly. Do the following:

- Set the polling interval set in the sender JDBC adapter.
- Write your query in the Sender JDBC adapter.

Refer to this thread "JDBC Sender Update Query".

https://www.sdn.sap.com/sdn/collaboration.sdn?contenttype=url&content=https%3A//forums.sdn.sap.com/thread.jspa%3FforumID%3D44%26threadID%3D44888%26messageID%3D453944%23453944

Question 43: IDoc and HTTP Adapters - Sender Agreement

I understand that we don't need to use sender agreement for IDoc and HTTP adapters, because they are sitting right on the ABAP stack. But we do use receiver adapter and receiver agreements even though these two adapters are on ABAP stack.

Can you give an explanation or a link that can explain this clearly?

A: Sender agreement for IDoc and HTTP adapters can be created because sometimes we need to. This is if we want to use Adapter-Specific Message Attributes for the http adapter, for example.

The following link explains why we use sender agreements (security, adapter attributes, etc.) Specifically, check the section on Obligatory Sender Agreements.

http://help.sap.com/saphelp_nw04/helpdata/en/b1/f29e7a56e18a439984a3c6630951d2/content.htm

This links tells where exactly Idoc adapter comes into picture; also architecture.

http://help.sap.com/saphelp_nw04/helpdata/en/ab/bdb13b00ae793be10000000a11402f/content.htm

And this, for HTTP (read last 2 paragraphs of the section on Integration).

http://help.sap.com/saphelp_nw04/helpdata/en/44/79973cc73af456e10000000a114084/content.htm

Question 44: Receiver JDBC Adapter

My scenario is an R/3 to XI to JDBC. When any error is encountered in the receiver end, will the JDBC adapter retry ?

There is no error on the XI part. In RWB to Communication channel monitoring, I got the error (I simulated the error by giving wrong database/table name).

The msg in Commn. channel monitoring is:

Error while parsing or executing XML-SQL document: Error processing request in sax parser: Error when executing statement for table/stored proc. 'Employee'(structure 'STATEMENTNAME'): java.sql.SQLException: [SQL0204] Employee in SARJAI type *FILE not found.
8/30/06 1:15:36 PM 44f4a7b2b2c417ce01000000ac130c39

Processing started.

I expected to get the message only once, but I got it four times. The interface got triggered only once and there is only 1 message in SXMB_MONI.

I didn't know why it happened? Can you please explain?

A: The most probable reason for the error occurring four times is that the IS_Retry parameter was set to 4 times.

The parameter QRFC_RESTART_ALLOWED is used to restart the queues if it is stuck for whatever reasons.

All messages will go thru this message queues in XI. Once adapter puts messages in the integration engine, it will be in message queues. It is administrated in the transaction code SXMB_ADM->Manage Queues.

Question 45: AE_DETAILS_ GET_ERROR

I tried to configure an HTTP to XI to mail scenario. I got the following error in SXMB_MONI:


```
<?xml version="1.0" encoding="UTF-8" standalone="yes" ?>
- <!-- Call Adapter
-->
- <SAP:Error xmlns:SAP="http://sap.com/xi/XI/Message/30"
xmlns:SOAP="http://schemas.xmlsoap.org/soap/envelope/"
SOAP:mustUnderstand="1">
<SAP:Category>XIServer</SAP:Category>
<SAP:Code
area="INTERNAL">AE_DETAILS_GET_ERROR</SAP:Code>
<SAP:P1>af.xid.sap1</SAP:P1>
<SAP:P2 />
<SAP:P3 />
<SAP:P4 />
<SAP:AdditionalText>3: Unable to find URL for Adapter Engine
af.xid.sap1</SAP:AdditionalText>
<SAP:ApplicationFaultMessage namespace="" />
<SAP:Stack>Error when reading the access data (URL, user, password)
for the Adapter Engine af.xid.sap1</SAP:Stack>
<SAP:Retry>M</SAP:Retry>
</SAP:Error>
```


I am not sure, whether this is related to sender HTTP or receiver Mail adapter.

Can you give any solution to this?

A: Some websites can be accessed only if you disable your firewall or configure it correctly to handle the transactions with the said websites.

Normally, this error occurs because of your adapter engine has a case sensitive issue.

MAPPING

Question 46: Multi mapping

Will multi mapping always produce 2 or more target messages?

Based on some source message, I need to decide the target mapping, say field "Receiver" in source. If the value is "1", I need to map the source with target1 message and if the value is 2 I need to map the source with target2 message. Is this possible?

A: The scenario you mentioned can be done using multi mapping. Multi mapping is when multiple messages are involved in the mapping in either the source or the target.

Check for the condition and then create the target mapping. You will need to check for the condition for every field of the target during mapping though.

As your target field creation depends on some condition, you will have to make the check against the source field for every target field.

Question 47: Graphical Mapping

I created a mapping between my file structures to the BAPI structure. This is actually the file that will call BAPI for 1: N (file having various headers and line items, each header and associated line items will be able to call BAPI in target side).

I tested the said mapping, but the following error came when I checked in the Interface Mapping.

ERROR: Mapping program Message Mapping MM_request | urn:testing does not match the interface mapping. The number or frequencies of source or target messages for the message mapping are not identical to the number or frequencies of source or target interfaces.

But when I did the test in the MM editor using duplicate subtree, it works fine.

I did the mapping like this:

```
Sourcefilestructure: TargetBAPI
-----------------------------------------
Messages (1:1) Message(1:1)
Message1(1:1) Message1(1:1)
MT_Request(1:1)
Recordset(0:U) --> BAPI_INCOMINGINVOICE(0:U)
HDR (0:1) HeaderData(1:1)
Filed(0:1) --> filed1(0:1)
Field(0:1) --> field2(0:2)
HDR---> GLACCOUNTDATA(0:1)
LINEITEM(0:U)---> item(0:U)
field1(0:1) ---> field(0:1)
field2(0:1) ---> field2(0:1)
```

Can you give me any idea where I made the error?

A: You are doing your multi mapping right and you have changed the occurrences in the message tab in the message mapping.

Check if you changed the occurrences in the interface mapping. The reason for this is because in the last column, there is an occurrence.

You will have this kind of error message when inside your Interface Mapping you used occurrences which are NOT the one defined in your Message Mapping.

In your message mapping, look at the tab "Message" and keep in mind the occurrences.

Then in your Interface Mapping, do the same action and compare both occurrences.

Question 48: Unlock a Message Mapping

I work remote via VPN on my XI server. The VPN was suddenly disconnected while I was working on a message mapping. After reconnecting and restarting the repository, I tried to work on the message mapping again, but XI open a dialog with the information that the mapping is already in work by my user.

Where can I unlock this?

A: You will have to go to the XI Home Page, then access 'Administration', then 'Lock Overview', and then unlock your objects.

If you want detailed information on this, visit:

http://server:port/rep/support/public/LockAdminService

Question 49: N:1 Mapping Possible using Java Mapping

Is it possible to do an N:1 mapping using Java Mapping? If possible, how?

The reason for this question is that the 'execute()' of the Java Mapping is going to take the source / request message as the Input Stream. In the case of N:1 mapping, as we have multiple messages, how will they be sent to the Input Stream? Will both the messages be sent combined into theInput Stream? Will the MESSAGE tag be embedded into the input stream?

A: Yes, it is possible to do an N: 1 mapping using Java Mapping.

For multiple messages, XI's input stream will be something like:

```
<ns0:Messages xmlns:ns0="http://sap.com/xi/XI/SplitAndMerge">
<ns0:Message1>
<YOURXML1>...</YOURXML1>
</ns0:Message1>
<ns0:Message2>
<YOURXML2>...</YOURXML2>
</ns0:Message2>
<ns0:Messages>
```

So, your root tag will be messages and inside each "messageX" you will find your input messages exactly like the source code for the source messages in Interface Mapping test tab.

This approach works for both Java and XSLT multi mappings.

Question 50: Mapping Test

What is the difference between “Test Tab under Message Mapping” and “Test Tab under Interface Mapping”?

A: “Test Tab under message mapping” can be used test only graphical mapping. It is a test at message level.

“Test tab under interface mapping” can test XSLT / Graphical / Java. This test is at interface level.

For more details concerning this discussion, visit the following links.

Message Mapping Test

http://help.sap.com/saphelp_nw04/helpdata/en/c3/e3072e65f04445a010847aa970b68b/content.htm

Interface Mapping Test

http://help.sap.com/saphelp_nw04/helpdata/en/db/860f1ee5f945d699a717cd9b4512a7/content.htm

Question 51: "No steps" Mapping & Determination in Pipeline (SXMB_MONI)

I'm using a SAP/R3 IDoc->XI->IDoc SAP/R3 with IDoc RSINFO. All is fine and works well.

But in SXMB_MONI, I don't see pipeline steps:

- Receiver determination
- Interface determination

I only see:

- Inbound message (central)
- Receiver grouping
- Response

Is there any way of customizing to log and see those steps?

A: To specifically see all the logging desired in SXMB_MONI, use SXMB_ADM and set the following flags to "1";

category/parameter
RUNTIME/LOGGING
RUNTIME/LOGGING_PROPAGATION
RUNTIME/LOGGING_SYNC

These logging parameters should be set only on DEV systems, as they will introduce additional disk space requirement.

Check this blog for additional information.

https://weblogs.sdn.sap.com/pub/wlg/1629

Question 52: Mapping Flat Structure in Complex Structure

Is it possible to use graphical mapping to obtain the following result?

I have this example input message type:

```
<?xml version="1.0" encoding="UTF-8"?>
<ns0:MT_CONFERMA xmlns:ns0="http://prova">
<HEADER>
<TRASM>1</TRASM>
<MDI>1234</MDI>
</HEADER>
<HEADER>
<TRASM>2</TRASM>
<MDI>2657</MDI>
</HEADER>
<ROW>
<TRASM>1</TRASM>
<RNUM>1.1</RNUM>
<ART>1.1</ART>
</ROW>
<ROW>
<TRASM>1</TRASM>
<RNUM>1.2</RNUM>
<ART>1.2</ART>
</ROW>
<ROW>
<TRASM>2</TRASM>
<RNUM>2.1</RNUM>
<ART>2.1</ART>
</ROW>
<ROW>
<TRASM>2</TRASM>
<RNUM>2.2</RNUM>
<ART>2.2</ART>
</ROW>
</ns0:MT_CONFERMA>
```

Result:

```
<ns0:MT_OUT xmlns:ns0="http://prova">
<DATA>
<TRASM>1</TRASM>
<MDI>1234</MDI>
<ROW>
<TRASM>1</TRASM>
<RNUM>1.1</RNUM>
<ART>1.1</ART>
</ROW>
<ROW>
<TRASM>1</TRASM>
<RNUM>1.2</RNUM>
<ART>1.2</ART>
</ROW>
</DATA>
<DATA>
<TRASM>2</TRASM>
<MDI>2657</MDI>
<ROW>
<TRASM>2</TRASM>
<RNUM>2.1</RNUM>
<ART>2.1</ART>
</ROW>
<ROW>
<TRASM>2</TRASM>
<RNUM>2.2</RNUM>
<ART>2.2</ART>
</ROW>
</DATA>
</ns0:MT_OUT>
```

The split data is "TRASM". I tried some methods but without the correct solution.

Can you help me solve this?

A: Yes. Apply this correction:

CONFERMA - > MT_OUT
HEADER -> DATA
TRASM - >TRASM
MDI - >MDI

ROW:

TRASM (cont. CONFERMA)- >split(byvalue-value change)ROW
RNUM- >RNUM
ART->ART

Question 53: XI XML to IDoc Mapping

I have a scenario where I have an XML to IDoc mapping. I have an XML sent from an SCM system & IDoc is getting converted in the XI but the IDoc that is getting created in the R/3 does not have the data that is contained in the XML. The control structure in the IDoc do not have the message variant populated in the IDoc, whereas in the SXMB_MONI, I could see the IDoc (XML format) containing this data.

The system has the note 886263 implemented. Can I check the XML within the R/3 system?

A: You will need to check these things first.

1. Is the control record fields filled up or not in the R/3 system?
2. Do you want to manipulate the Control Record from XI? Have you selected the option, Apply Control Record from payload, take sender from payload, take receiver from payload in the IDoc adapter?

Your control structure must have been partially filled with the message type but the message variant is not filled in the XI.

You may need to enable the check box for the Apply control record values for the payload for it to work.

You can pick some pointers in this blog:

https://weblogs.sdn.sap.com/pub/wlg/2279

Question 54: Defining Content Conversion and Mapping

We have a situation where a flat file looks somewhat like the following:
name,age
city,country
id,number
dept,wing

Now in the flat file, the input may vary as shown below:
name,age
city,country
id,number
dept,wing
name1,age1
city1,country1
id1,number1
dept1,wing1

Or:
name,age
city,country
id,number
dept,wing
name1,age1
city1,country1
name2,age2
city2,country2

Or:
id,number
dept,wing
id1,number1
dept1,wing1
name,age
city,country

Or:
name,age
city,country
name1,age1
city1,country1

Or:
id,number
dept,wing
id1,number1
dept1,wing1

In short, the <name,age> will always be followed by <city,country> and <id,number> by <dept,wing> but the combinations occur in random, for example, <name,age> & <city,country> may come before the <id,number> & <dept,wing> or vice versa.

We do make use of key fields. But when the combinations occur in random, how do we define its content conversion and mapping?

A: The answer lies in defining the source data type. It may look something like this:

```
Dt_input
|
Details (0-Unbounded)
|_title (0-Unbounded)
|_name
|_age
|_info(0-Unbounded)
|_city
|_country
|_tag(0-Unbounded)
|_id
|_number
|_node(0-Unbounded)
|_dept
|_wing
```

During content conversion, treat the recordset as details and the recordset structure as title,*,info,*,tag,*,node,*;. You can also specify the recordset per message as *.

Question 55: Mapping Problem

I was working on a scenario file to R/3. I got the error message in SXMB_MONI as:

"mapping exception during execute"

I checked the mapping in IR to Mapping test. The result message is:

```
Messages:
13:16:40 Start of test
Unparseable date: "06.04."
com.sap.aii.utilxi.misc.api.BaseRuntimeException: Unparseable date:
"06.04."
at
com.sap.aii.mappingtool.flib3.DateTransformer.convertDate(DateTrans
former.ja
va:39)
at
com.sap.aii.mappingtool.flib3.DateTransformer.getValue(DateTransfor
mer.java:
27)
at
com.sap.aii.mappingtool.tf3.AMappingProgram.processNode(AMappi
ngProgram.java
:369)
at
com.sap.aii.mappingtool.tf3.AMappingProgram.processNode(AMappi
ngProgram.java
:387)
at
com.sap.aii.mappingtool.tf3.AMappingProgram.processNode(AMappi
ngProgram.java
:387)
at
com.sap.aii.mappingtool.tf3.AMappingProgram.processNode(AMappi
ngProgram.java
:387)
at
```

```
com.sap.aii.mappingtool.tf3.AMappingProgram.start(AMappingProgra
m.java:287)
at
com.sap.aii.mappingtool.tf3.Transformer.start(Transformer.java:63)
at
com.sap.aii.mappingtool.tf3.AMappingProgram.execute(AMappingPro
gram.java:232
)
at
com.sap.aii.ibrep.server.mapping.ServerMapService.transformInternal(
ServerMa
pService.java:432)
at
com.sap.aii.ibrep.server.mapping.ServerMapService.execute(ServerMa
pService.j
ava:170)
at
com.sap.aii.ibrep.sbeans.mapping.MapServiceBean.execute(MapServic
eBean.java:
52)
at
com.sap.aii.ibrep.sbeans.mapping.MapServiceRemoteObjectImpl0.exe
cute(MapServ
iceRemoteObjectImpl0.java:259)
at
com.sap.aii.ibrep.sbeans.mapping.MapServiceRemoteObjectImpl0p4_
Skel.dispatch
(MapServiceRemoteObjectImpl0p4_Skel.java:146)
at
com.sap.engine.services.rmi_p4.DispatchImpl._runInternal(DispatchIm
pl.java:2
94)
at
com.sap.engine.services.rmi_p4.DispatchImpl._run(DispatchImpl.java:
183)
at
com.sap.engine.services.rmi_p4.server.P4SessionProcessor.request(P4
SessionPr
ocessor.java:119)
at
com.sap.engine.core.service630.context.cluster.session.ApplicationSess
ionMes
sageListener.process(ApplicationSessionMessageListener.java:37)
```

```
at
com.sap.engine.core.cluster.impl6.session.UnorderedChannel$Message
Runner.run
(UnorderedChannel.java:71)
at
com.sap.engine.core.thread.impl3.ActionObject.run(ActionObject.java:
37)
at java.security.AccessController.doPrivileged(Native Method)
at
com.sap.engine.core.thread.impl3.SingleThread.execute(SingleThread.j
ava:95)
at
com.sap.engine.core.thread.impl3.SingleThread.run(SingleThread.java:
159)
Root Cause:
java.text.ParseException: Unparseable date: "06.04."
at java.text.DateFormat.parse(DateFormat.java:335)
at
com.sap.aii.mappingtool.flib3.DateTransformer.convertDate(DateTrans
former.ja
va:35)
at
com.sap.aii.mappingtool.flib3.DateTransformer.getValue(DateTransfor
mer.java:
27)
at
com.sap.aii.mappingtool.tf3.AMappingProgram.processNode(AMappi
ngProgram.java
:369)
at
com.sap.aii.mappingtool.tf3.AMappingProgram.processNode(AMappi
ngProgram.java
:387)
at
com.sap.aii.mappingtool.tf3.AMappingProgram.processNode(AMappi
ngProgram.java
:387)
at
com.sap.aii.mappingtool.tf3.AMappingProgram.processNode(AMappi
ngProgram.java
:387)
at
```

```
com.sap.aii.mappingtool.tf3.AMappingProgram.start(AMappingProgra
m.java:287)
at
com.sap.aii.mappingtool.tf3.Transformer.start(Transformer.java:63)
at
com.sap.aii.mappingtool.tf3.AMappingProgram.execute(AMappingPro
gram.java:232
)
at
com.sap.aii.ibrep.server.mapping.ServerMapService.transformInternal(
ServerMa
pService.java:432)
at
com.sap.aii.ibrep.server.mapping.ServerMapService.execute(ServerMa
pService.j
ava:170)
at
com.sap.aii.ibrep.sbeans.mapping.MapServiceBean.execute(MapServic
eBean.java:
52)
at
com.sap.aii.ibrep.sbeans.mapping.MapServiceRemoteObjectImpl0.exe
cute(MapServ
iceRemoteObjectImpl0.java:259)
at
com.sap.aii.ibrep.sbeans.mapping.MapServiceRemoteObjectImpl0p4_
Skel.dispatch
(MapServiceRemoteObjectImpl0p4_Skel.java:146)
at
com.sap.engine.services.rmi_p4.Dis patchImpl._runInternal(DispatchIm
pl.java:2
94)
at
com.sap.engine.services.rmi_p4.DispatchImpl._run(DispatchImpl.java:
183)
at
com.sap.engine.services.rmi_p4.server.P4SessionProcessor.request(P4
SessionPr
ocessor.java:119)
at
com.sap.engine.core.service630.context.cluster.session.ApplicationSess
ionMes
sageListener.process(ApplicationSessionMessageListener.java:37)
```

at
com.sap.engine.core.cluster.impl6.session.UnorderedChannel$MessageRunner.run
(UnorderedChannel.java:71)
at
com.sap.engine.core.thread.impl3.ActionObject.run(ActionObject.java:37)
at java.security.AccessController.doPrivileged(Native Method)
at
com.sap.engine.core.thread.impl3.SingleThread.execute(SingleThread.java:95)
at
com.sap.engine.core.thread.impl3.SingleThread.run(SingleThread.java:159)
13:16:40 End of test

Can you give me some pointers in fixing this?

A: There is a date value which your codes were not able to parse. Check if you are using any user defined functions.

Unparseable date:
"06.04."

This is due to some date transformation problem. Use the correct format;

dd.mm.yyyy or mm.dd.yyyy

For better debugging, you can check the Display Queue option in the Message Mapping in the IR. Check each input values.

You will need to check the input XML. Is this a valid XML? You can check this by saving into notepad with .xml and open in the browser. You can also use XML editors.

Question 56: Mapping Specific Elements to Generic Elements

I need to map source specific elements into target generic elements which are specialized with a "name" attribute. I don't know how I can specify at the same time the "name" attribute's value ("currency" or "edi_currency" for example) depending on the present source elements (CURCY, HWAER, and KUNDEUINR) and copy this source element's value as the target element's value.

This is an example:

Source:

```
<ORDERS05>
<IDOC>
<E1EDK01>
<CURCY>XXX</CURCY>
<HWAER>YYY</HWAER>
<KUNDEUINR>ZZZ</KUNDEUINR>
...
</E1EDK01>
</IDOC>
</ORDERS05>
```

Target:

```
<MYORDER>
<HEADER>
<PROP name="currency">XXX</PROP>
<PROP name="edi_currency">YYY</PROP>
<PROP name="vat_reg_nbr">ZZZ</PROP>
...
</HEADER>
</MYORDER>
```

Can this be done? If so, how?

A: You can do your mapping with standard graphical mapping features. There is no need for a user defined function. A simple "How to" will suffice:

1. Do this mapping:

   CURCY --> PROP
   Constant[currency] -->@name

2. Duplicate the structure PROP. Right click mouse and pick duplicate subtree and map the second occurrence of PROP as follows:

   HWAER --> PROP
   Constant[edi_currency] --> @name

3. Duplicate the structure PROP again and map the third occurrence as follows:

   KUNDEUINR --> PROP
   Constant[vat_reg_nbr] --> @name

You can also check the following blog on how to duplicate subtrees.

https://www.sdn.sap.com/irj/sdn/weblogs?blog=/pub/wlg/4052

Question 57: Java Mapping Error

We have saved java maps in zip files. We are getting the following error when we tried to test it.

```
14:29:25 Start of test
LinkageError at JavaMapping.load(): Could not load class:
build/classes/com/bmwmc/pcard/mapping/Response

java.lang.NoClassDefFoundError:
build/classes/com/bmwmc/pcard/mapping/Response (wrong name:
com/bmwmc/pcard/mapping/Response)
at java.lang.ClassLoader.defineClass0(Native Method)
at java.lang.ClassLoader.defineClass(ClassLoader.java:539)
at java.lang.ClassLoader.defineClass(ClassLoader.java:448)
at
com.sap.aii.ibrep.server.mapping.ibrun.RepMappingLoader.findClass(
RepMappingLoader.java:175)
at java.lang.ClassLoader.loadClass(ClassLoader.java:289)
at java.lang.ClassLoader.loadClass(ClassLoader.java:235)
at
com.sap.aii.ibrep.server.mapping.ibrun.RepJavaMapping.load(RepJava
Mapping.java:136)
at
com.sap.aii.ibrep.server.mapping.ibrun.RepJavaMapping.execute(RepJ
avaMapping.java:50)
at
com.sap.aii.ibrep.server.mapping.ibrun.RepMappingHandler.run(RepM
appingHandler.java:75)
at
com.sap.aii.ibrep.server.mapping.rt.MappingHandlerAdapter.run(Mapp
ingHandlerAdapter.java:107)
at
com.sap.aii.ibrep.server.mapping.ServerMapService.transformInterface
Mapping(ServerMapService.java:127)
at
com.sap.aii.ibrep.server.mapping.ServerMapService.transform(Server
MapService.java:104)
at
com.sap.aii.ibrep.sbeans.mapping.MapServiceBean.transform(MapServ
iceBean.java:40)
```

at
com.sap.aii.ibrep.sbeans.mapping.MapServiceRemoteObjectImpl0.tran
sform(MapServiceRemoteObjectImpl0.java:131)
at
com.sap.aii.ibrep.sbeans.mapping.MapServiceRemoteObjectImpl0p4_
Skel.dispatch(MapServiceRemoteObjectImpl0p4_Skel.java:104)
at
com.sap.engine.services.rmi_p4.DispatchImpl._runInternal(DispatchIm
pl.java:294)
at
com.sap.engine.services.rmi_p4.DispatchImpl._run(DispatchImpl.java:
183)
at
com.sap.engine.services.rmi_p4.server.P4SessionProcessor.request(P4
SessionProcessor.java:119)
at
com.sap.engine.core.service630.context.cluster.session.ApplicationSess
ionMessageListener.process(ApplicationSessionMessageListener.java:
33)
at
com.sap.engine.core.cluster.impl6.session.MessageRunner.run(Messag
eRunner.java:41)
at
com.sap.engine.core.thread.impl3.ActionObject.run(ActionObject.java:
37)
at java.security.AccessController.doPrivileged(Native Method)
at
com.sap.engine.core.thread.impl3.SingleThread.execute(SingleThread.j
ava:95)
at
com.sap.engine.core.thread.impl3.SingleThread.run(SingleThread.java:
159)

14:29:25 End of test

Is there any way I can fix this?

A: You need to set the directory structure starting with com in your zip file and not with build/classes for the class files. So your zip has com/bmwmc/pcard/mapping/Response.class instead of build/classes/com/bmwmc/pcard/mapping/Response.

Question 58: RFC to Webservice Interface in XI

I am calling a web service hosted in the Internet from RFC (in SAP R/3) via XI. I have completed the design and configuration activities. But, while I execute the RFC I am getting a short dump with the message:

"call to messaging system failed: com.sap.aii.af.ra.ms.api.DeliveryException:".

I had created a sender Communication Channel (type RFC) giving a Program ID. Same Program ID is used in the TCP/IP RFC Destination in R/3. I checked the RFC destination and it is working fine. SAP XI engine is also activated.

I am using two synchronous message interfaces. The outbound interface is RFC and the inbound interface is webservice. I am getting two messages with Red flag in SXMB_MONI. I checked the run-time workbench and got the following error message:

Received XI System Error. ErrorCode: EXCEPTION_DURING_EXECUTE ErrorText: ErrorStack: During the application mapping com/sap/xi/tf/_MM_Webservice_OutputMap_ a com.sap.aii.utilxi.misc.api.BaseRuntimeException was thrown: Fatal Error: com.sap.engine.lib.xml.parser.Parser~
2006-07-28 11:30:54 Error Returning synchronous error notification to calling application: Application:EXCEPTION_DURING_EXECUTE:.
2006-07-28 11:30:54 Error Transmitting the message using connection http://ntbomsap11:8000/sap/xi/engine?type=entry failed, due to: Application:EXCEPTION_DURING_EXECUTE:.
2006-07-28 11:30:54 Error The message status s et to FAIL.

Can you please tell me why this is happening?

A: There are some problems in your message mapping. Just check if your Webservice_OutputMap have the correct structure. A simple guide "XI: How to test your mapping (in real life scenarios)" can be found at:

https://www.sdn.sap.com/irj/sdn/weblogs?blog=/pub/wlg/237 4

Question 59: ERROR: EXCEPTION_DURING_EXECUTE while using FILE CONTENT CONVERSION

I set up a file to file scenario with File Content Conversion for Sender communication channel. But I got the following error in SXMB_MONI.

```
<SAP:Category>Application</SAP:Category>
<SAP:Code
area="MAPPING">EXCEPTION_DURING_EXECUTE</SAP:Code>
<SAP:P1>com/sap/xi/tf/_MM_ContentBased_</SAP:P1>
<SAP:P2>com.sap.aii.utilxi.misc.api.BaseRuntimeException</SAP:P2
>
<SAP:P3>RuntimeException in Message-Mapping
transformatio~</SAP:P3>
<SAP:P4 />
<SAP:AdditionalText />
<SAP:ApplicationFaultMessage namespace="" />
<SAP:Stack>During the application mapping
com/sap/xi/tf/_MM_ContentBased_ a
com.sap.aii.utilxi.misc.api.BaseRuntimeException was thrown:
RuntimeException in Message-Mapping transformatio~</SAP:Stack>
<SAP:Retry>M</SAP:Retry>
</SAP:Error>
```

I tried the same message mapping for normal file to file scenario without using File Content Conversion. It went through fine.

Our file structure follows:

```
<Header>
<Sysnum>01</Sysnum>
</Header>
<Body>
<Name>ABCDE</Name>
<Age>25</Age>
<Stream>XYZ</Stream>
</Body>
```

The Sender Communication Channel Parameters follows:

Recordset Str: Header,1,Body,1

Header.fieldFixedLengths : 2

Header.fieldNames : Sysnum

Body.fieldFixedLengths : 5,2,3

Body.fieldNames : Name,Age,Stream

ignoreRecordsetName : true

How do I make this work?

A: Your message mapping failed. To rectify this, copy the XML message from monitoring and execute the mapping in Integration Builder with maximal trace to get the reason for the failure. From there, it would be easier to plot out corrections.

SENDER & RECEIVER ISSUES

Question 60: RFC Sender Problem (Asynchronous)

Is there a way to detect from a RFC FM asynchronous call if XI is down?

I understand that if the RFC call is asynchronous, no exceptions are caught. But is there a workaround on catching the error?

A: You can use transaction SM58 to restart LUW on your source system. In this transaction you will see all errors in asynchronous RFC communication.

Question 61: Error when Sending Null Records in BPM

In my scenario, I have four (4) Business systems involved.

1. File (Sender)
2. An Oracle DB (Receiver)
3. R3 (Receiver)
4. File (Receiver)

I used a File to R3 (using RFC) Scenario where I have a BPM. In XI, I did some validations and if any of the validations fail, I have to send those error records to a database table (System B). If the records pass the validation, it is sent to R3 (System C) and the count of the successfully updated records (in R3) are sent to System D.

In my BPM, I sent all correct records. There are no error records (no data to be passed to DB).

I got the following error.


```
<?xml version="1.0" encoding="UTF-8" standalone="yes" ?>
- <!-- Receiver Identification
-->
- <SAP:Error xmlns:SAP="http://sap.com/xi/XI/Message/30"
xmlns:SOAP="http://schemas.xmlsoap.org/soap/envelope/"
SOAP:mustUnderstand="">
<SAP:Category>XIServer</SAP:Category>
<SAP:Code
area="RCVR_DETERMINATION">MESSAGE_INCOMPLETE</SA
P:Code>
<SAP:P1>Sender</SAP:P1>
<SAP:P2 />
<SAP:P3 />
<SAP:P4 />
<SAP:AdditionalText />
<SAP:ApplicationFaultMessage namespace="" />
<SAP:Stack>Message is incomplete. No Sender found</SAP:Stack>
<SAP:Retry>M</SAP:Retry>
</SAP:Error>
```

The scenario works fine when there are records to be sent to DB.

I used multi mapping in my scenario. Steps in my BPM are:

1. Receive step.
2. Transformation Step
3. Block (For Each)
4. Inside the block I have a switch step to do the check (validation).
5. In my first branch I appended the correct records to a multi-line container.
6. In the other branch I appended the error messages to a multi-line container.
7. Outside the block I have a transformation step for bundling the error records and a send step for sending the error records.
8. Next I have another transformation step for bundling the correct records and a send step for sending the correct records. This is a synchronous send step for getting response from R3.
9. And then, the final send step for sending the count.

Can you tell me if there is any other option available for such a scenario, because I may have null records for errors? Is there any error handling mechanism available which I can use here?

A: You can actually create the message type and check the flag using a fork or a switch. If it is a valid payload, let it go through the same step; otherwise, don't.

An alternate yet a similar scenario:

1. Receive
2. Transformation (receiver MT, audit MT and error MT all done in one MM)
3. Switch (to check valid condition for sending receiver MT, audit MT and error MT)
4. Block inside switch for each condition and send step in the block.

Question 62: Receiver Determination Step in BPM

I have a BPM process similar to 'Multicat BPM Pattern'. I have some questions regarding how the 'Receiver Determination' works:

1. Does it have to have interface determination in the 'Integration Directory'?
2. Does that interface determination (including the mapping) takes place when sending a message to a receiver from that 'Receiver Determination' step, or should I perform a 'Mapping' step explicitly in the process?

Example:

My source message is A. My receiver requires the message B.

If I define a 'Receiver Determination', and a corresponding 'Interface Determination', which maps the source message A to the message B, and then I use a send step to a receiver from that 'Receiver Determination', do I need to send the message A or the message B?

A:

1. In every 'Receiver Determination', you need to have an 'Interface Determination'.

   Example is given here:

   http://help.sap.com/saphelp_nw2004s/helpdata/en/14/d5283fd0ca8443e10000000a114084/content.htm

2. Receiver From: Receivers List

   It just sends message (A) to the receiver, or also performs the mapping.

If you have given / selected the appropriate 'INTERFACE MAPPING' for 'Interface Determination', then mapping will be performed.

If you have not selected Interface Mapping, then the mapping will not be performed.

Question 63: RFC Receiver

We have a RFC receiver adapter pointing to a client. We want it to point to another R/3 client.

Is it enough to change the adapter specific information regarding the receiver?

A: Yes, the adapter specific information is enough to change the receiver settings.

For more information, visit the following links:

http://help.sap.com/saphelp_nw04/helpdata/en/33/c6e63b60c25767e10000000a11402f/content.htm

http://help.sap.com/saphelp_nw04/helpdata/en/c8/e80440a832e369e10000000a155106/content.htm

Question 64: JDBC Receiver Document Format

I have to pull the data from DB. The SQL Query is:

Select field1
from systemName.table
where field2 = field1
order by field1.

Can you help me find a way to define the data type to realize the SQL query on the receiver side?

A: You will need to import this ".xsd" as external definition and then proceed.

```
<xsd:schema elementFormDefault="qualified"
xmlns:xsd="http://www.w3.org/2001/XMLSchema">
<xsd:element name="Receiver_JDBC" type="Statement1"/>
<xsd:complexType name="Statement1">
<xsd:sequence>
<xsd:element name="statement1">
<xsd:complexType>
<xsd:sequence>
<xsd:element name="Vishal">
<xsd:complexType>
<xsd:sequence>
<xsd:element name="access"/>
<xsd:element name="key">
<xsd:complexType>
<xsd:sequence></xsd:sequence>
</xsd:complexType>
</xsd:element>
</xsd:sequence>
<xsd:attribute name="action">
<xsd:simpleType>
<xsd:restriction base="xsd:string">
<xsd:pattern value="SQL_QUERY|SQL_DML"/>
</ xsd:restriction>
</xsd:simpleType>
</xsd:attribute>
</xsd:complexType>
```

```
</xsd:element>
</xsd:sequence>
</xsd:complexType>
</xsd:element>
</xsd:sequence>
</xsd:complexType>
</xsd:schema>
```

You can generate this ".xsd" using XML spy or any other XML tool.

You can use "SQL_QUERY" or "SQL_DML", but you loose the dynamic of your request.

I would recommend you to use action "SELECT" like describe in library. The problem is the clause "order by", can't be solved this way in JDBC adapter, but easy with an (additional) XSLT mapping.

Use element xsl:sort as child from xsl:apply-templates or xsl:for-each. Use if necessary, attribute orders with values ascending or descending. Use may be attribute data-type with values "number"/"text".

Question 65: Unable to Determine Receiver

I got a problem in Receiver Determination. The error is generated at the Receiver Grouping tag in SXMB_MONI. The error description is "Unable to Determine receiver (processing type:QOS = EO or EOIO)".

Below is the trace snippet where the error is getting generated.

<Trace level="1" type="System_Error">Exit XMB because of system error!</Trace>
<Trace level="3" type="System_Error">System-Error: ROUTING.NO_RECEIVER_CASE_ASYNC</Trace>
<Trace level="3" type="System_Error">Unable to determine a receiver (processing type: QoS = EO or EOIO)</Trace>
<Trace level="1" type="Timestamp">2004-08-05T16:36:52ZEnd of pipeline service processing PLSRVID= PLSRV_RECEIVER_DETERMINATION</Trace>

Can you help me correct this problem?

A: You need to check if you have created namespace correctly.

Verify if you have the namespace created with "http://..." and not "http:\\...." Do not use this slash (\) or backslash, as the system considers it as an escape character and therefore it does not work.

Question 66: JDBC Receiver Action Select

I have this problem with a JDBC Receiver Adapter. I want to make a synchronize process form a Web service to TeraData Database. The deployed driver works and I can get Data with JDBC Sender Adapter, but I get this error:

```
<?xml version="1.0" encoding="UTF-8" standalone="yes" ?>
- <!-- Aufruf eines Adapters
-->
- <SAP:Error xmlns:SAP="http://sap.com/xi/XI/Message/30"
xmlns:SOAP="http://schemas.xmlsoap.org/soap/envelope/"
SOAP:mustUnderstand="1">
<SAP:Category>XIAdapterFramework</SAP:Category>
<SAP:Code area="MESSAGE">GENERAL</SAP:Code>
<SAP:P1 />
<SAP:P2 />
<SAP:P3 />
<SAP:P4 />
<SAP:AdditionalText>comsap.aii.af.ra.ms.api.DeliveryException:
Error processing request in sax parser: No 'action' attribute found in
XML document (attribute "action" missing or wrong XML
structure)</SAP:AdditionalText>
<SAP:ApplicationFaultMessage namespace="" />
<SAP:Stack />
<SAP:Retry>M</SAP:Retry>
</SAP:Error>
```

But the structure is the same as on the sap help:

```
<M_VerlagSelect>
<verlag action="SELECT">
<table>verlag</table>
<access>
<Objekt />
<Objekt_Bezeichnung />
<Level />
</access>
<key1>
<Verlag>10000</Verlag>
<Level>O</Level>
```

```
</key1>
</pvg_usrObjekt>
</M_VerlagSelect>
```

JDBC Adapter Receiver

Can you help me fix this?

A: Yes. The problem is you have missed the STATEMENT tag,

```
<M_VerlagSelect>
<STATEMENT>
<verlag action="SELECT">
<table>verlag</table>
<access>
<Objekt />
<Objekt_Bezeichnung />
<Level />
</access>
<key1>
<Verlag>10000</Verlag>
<Level>O</Level>
</key1>
</pvg_usrObjekt>
</STATEMENT>
</M_VerlagSelect>
```

You have a tag </pvg_usrObjekt>. It should be either inside KEY 1 or KEY2 and so on.

For more details, visit;

https://weblogs.sdn.sap.com/pub/wlg/3928

Question 67: Configuration Error in Receiving SAP R/3

I configured a File to XI to R/3 (ABAP Proxy) scenario. When I checked in SXMB_MONI, it gave me an error in XI. The error ID I got in SXMB_MONI:

"SYSTEM_NOT_CONFIGURED_AS XMB".

Can you help me figure this out?

A: You need to go and check in the Receiving R/3 system.

Access the following:

SXMB_ADM, then Configuration, then Integration Engine Configuration, then choose your R/3 system as Application System.

For more details, visit the link at:

https://www.sdn.sap.com/irj/sdn/thread?forumID=44&threadID=62067&messageID=656136

Also refer to this Configuration Guide, page 27 of:

https://websmp102.sap-ag.de/~sapidb/011000358700001697502004E.PDF

And also check this web blog:

https://weblogs.sdn.sap.com/pub/wlg/3022

Question 68: Set Message's Party inside BPM

We have a scenario where a business system sends a message to XI, a BPM receives it, and depending on the value of a field, the BPM should determine the party where to send it.

I know how to obtain the Sender or Receiver Party in a transformation, but not how to set it.

How can I send the party to a message?

A: BPM does not send the message to the party. You have to define a receiver agreement for you BPM (your BPM is a service in ID).

So when BPM sends the message via a send step, the message goes from the workflow-engine to the integration engine.

There in the integration engine, the ID, and in your receiver determination, you can maintain conditions for the receivers.

Question 69: BPM or not?

I need to pull data from an Oracle database and query SAP table from the data pulled from Oracle. Based on the data from SAP, the data should be updated into the Oracle Database.

This has to happen on a daily basis at 7 am.

Should I go for a BPM or could it be done in an interface?

A: You definitely need to go for BPM. You need to use a sender JDBC adapter to pull in the data into XI.

Here are steps in using BPM:

1. Receive data from Oracle.
2. Send sync data to SAP.
3. Map the response from SAP to the DB for updating (receiver JDBC).

To run a BPM at a certain time, there's a couple of links I advise you to visit.

Scheduling BPM:

https://weblogs.sdn.sap.com/pub/wlg/1672

Scheduling the file adapter:

https://www.sdn.sap.com/irj/servlet/prt/portal/prtroot/docs/library/uuid/d458a870-0601-0010-caab-b99c79741964

Question 70: RFC Sends Data to an SQL Server

I'm trying to make a simple scenario where RFC sends data to an SQL server. I made all the mappings interfaces, etc. When I execute make a dump, an error:

"Server repository could not create a function template"

Can you help me correct this?

A: Make sure that you have defined the appropriate server settings for "RFC Metadata Repository" in the RFC Sender Adapter settings. It must point to a server where the function is defined. The sender adapter accesses the RFC metadata at runtime.

GENERAL XI CONFIGURATION

Question 71: Comparing Data from 2 Tables

This is a JDBC-Proxy scenario. I used a JDBC sender adapter to pick records from the table and used a proxy to pass the data to R/3 and called a function module in R/3. The scenario worked fine as expected.

There is another table in the database which contains the history. I need to compare the records in the 2 tables and pass the data to R/3 if a record does not exist in second table. But if a record exists, I need to check for the "amount" field again. If the amount in the history file is lesser, the record has to be passed with the amount (difference between the first table and history table). If the amount is also the same, I should not send the record to R/3.

How can I do these comparisons and then pass the data to R/3?

A: You need a BPM and you need to select the data from the database for the history table. Then do a mapping and determine whether IDoc is to be sent out or not. The steps are as follows:

1. Receive - select data from Table 1.
2. Send Sync - select data from table 2.
3. Transformation (n:1) - combine the data from step 1 and step 2 and do the mapping. Set a field to determine if the IDoc should be sent or not.
4. Switch - check for the data and then send the IDoc if needed, otherwise terminate the BPM and process flow.

For more detailed information, visit this link:

https://weblogs.sdn.sap.com/pub/wlg/3928

Question 72: Server Proxy not executed - Not updating Data

I am currently working on a File to XI to ECC 5.0 scenario. The message reached ECC side and the status in SXMB_MONI is filed and contained the payload. I have tested the proxy interface from SPROXY and it works fine (updating the database).

But in runtime it's not updating the database. It seems that it is not executing the method "EXECUTE_ASYNCHRONOUS". I was not able to see it in SM51 though it has an infinite loop.

Can you give some advice concerning this?

A: You need to go and check the error that shows in the SXMB_MONI of your ECC system. Make sure that queues are registered correctly in the ECC system. To do this, you need to access 'SXMB_ADM', then 'Manage Queues', then 'Register All'.

The link below can give you more detailed information.

https://www.sdn.sap.com/irj/sdn/weblogs?blog=/pub/wlg/2884

Question 73: File to XI to JDBC Error

I was processing a file to JDBC scenario which I took as an example from this link:

https://www.sdn.sap.com/irj/sdn/weblogs?blog=/pub/wlg/1772

I got the following error in the JDBC adapter monitoring:

Receiver Adapter v2606 for Party '', Service 'JDBC_Service': Configured at 16:31:32 2006-09-08 Last message processing started 16:47:07 2006-09-08, Error: TransformException error in xml processor class, rollback: Error processing request in sax parser: No 'action' attribute found in XML document (attribute "action" missing or wrong XML structure) SXMB_MONI says that the message has been processed successfully.

Here is my source XML (XI picks this xml file thru file adapter):

<p2:data_filesender_MT xmlns:p2="http://filetojdbc">
<EMPID>JDK</EMPID>
<EMPNAME>JohnDoe</EMPNAME>
<EMPAGE>3</EMPAGE>
<FLAG>Yes</FLAG>
</p2:data_filesender_MT>

Here is my target XML (in the message mapping test window):
<p2:data_jdbcreceiver_MT xmlns:p2="http://filetojdbc">
<STATEMENTNAME>
<Table1>
<action>INSERT</action>
<TABLE>Table1</TABLE>
<access>
<EMPID>JDK</EMPID>
<EMPNAME>JohnDoe</EMPNAME>
<EMPAGE>3</EMPAGE>
<FLAG>Yes</FLAG>
</access>
</Table1>
</STATEMENTNAME>
</p2:data_jdbcreceiver_MT>

Can you point to me what I did wrong?

A: You have created the ACTION as an element under TABLE. ACTION should be the ATTRIBUTE of the elements TABLE.

```
<p2:data_jdbcreceiver_MT xmlns:p2="http://filetojdbc">
<STATEMENTNAME>
<Table1 action ="INSERT">
<TABLE>Table1</TABLE>
<access>
<EMPID>JDK</EMPID>
<EMPNAME>JohnDoe</EMPNAME>
<EMPAGE>3</EMPAGE>
<FLAG>Yes</FLAG>
</access>
</Table1>
</STATEMENTNAME>
</p2:data_jdbcreceiver_MT>
```

Edit the 'datatype' and make ACTION an attribute and then use the constant INSERT.

Question 74: Handling Namespaces in XSLT xpaths

I'm trying to generate the SOAP envelope using XSLT mapping. The source message to my mapping program contains two fields:

1. Username
2. PWD

But they come in with attached namespaces like ns1.

How do I specify the xpath to get the data from them?

A: You need to put the namespace declaration into the style sheet element. For example,

```
<xsl:stylesheet version="1.0"
xmlns:xsl="http://www.w3.org/1999/XSL/Transform"
xmlns:ns1="namespace1">
```

Now you can select with:

```
<xsl:value-of select="//ns1:a.username"/>
```

Question 75: Distribute SAP HR Organizational Data via SAP XI

I have to distribute the HR (SAP ERP 2005) organizational data to a SAP CRM 5.0-system via XI. Is there only one standard technology using ALE/IDocs, or are there also some other technologies available?

As I would need to change a lot in the IDoc and the concerned BAPIs I would like to know if there are alternatives.

A: Yes, but IDocs/ALE is still the most popular interface with HR objects with ERP2005.

http://help.sap.com/saphelp_erp2005/helpdata/en/a8/ee2f37d7e21274e10000009b38f839/frameset.htm

Still, here are some options thru XI.

1. Use of IDocs
2. Use of RFCs/BAPIs
3. Use of Proxies

It depends on the availability of the function modules in the HR side. You can think of any one of the above methods to get the data into XI. If you want to customize the BAPIs, you can plan for developing proxy interface if feasible.

Question 76: RB_Split Option not found for Message Split

We are configuring to split a single XML with multiple records into multiple single record XML files. We have referenced the blog:

https://www.sdn.sap.com/irj/sdn/weblogs?blog=/pub/wlg/3115

During interface determination configuration, we cannot find the options for RB_Classic & RB_Split. We are on SPS17 already. Are we missing a patch of some sort? I can only see "Standard" and "Enhanced". I read somewhere that "Enhanced" is something completely different.

We already have the message mapping set up in IR. However, it looks like without this setting in ID, it is only performing the split once. So we only end up with the first record in the original message as output (5 records total).

We are simplifying our test to use 1 XML with 2 records and attempt to generate 2 single record XMLs. We are still only getting 1 output single record XML only. Our input XML looks like:

```
<ns0:MultiXML xmlns:ns0="urn:himax:b2bi:poc:multiMapTest">
<Record>
<ID>1</ID>
<FirstName>Steve</FirstName>
<LastName>Chen</LastName>
</Record>
<Record>
<ID>2</ID>
<FirstName>Sunny</FirstName>
<LastName>Huang</LastName>
</Record>
</ns0:MultiXML>
```

and desired output is:

<ns0:SingleXML>
<Record>
<ID>1</ID>
<FirstName>Steve</FirstName>
<LastName>Chen</LastName>
</Record>
</ns0:MultiXML>
... generate as many files as the original # of records.

For mapping, I have:

<MultiXML> 1..1 <SingleXML> 0..unbounded (no mapping)
<Record> 1..unbounded <---> <Record> 1..1
<ID> 1..1 <---> <ID> 1..1
etc. etc.

Is it something to do with our occurrence settings?

A: First, a clarification. If you choose ENHANCED in INTERFACE DETERMINATION, it is used for 1: N mapping.

There is also an ENHANCED option available in Receiver Determination from Sp16 onwards, which enables you to dynamically determine receivers using a mapping.

In your case, for 1: N mapping, choose ENHANCED in INTERFACE DETERMINATION.

Also, make sure that the occurrence of the MESSAGE TYPE and MESSAGE INTERFACE in MESSAGE MAPPING and INTERFACE MAPPING has been made 1 to unbounded.

For the mapping:

<MultiXML> 1..1 <SingleXML> 0..unbounded (no mapping)

This is the problem. Map it as follows:

1. RECORD of SOURCE should be mapped to <SINGLEXML> of target.

2. RECORD of target map it to a CONSTANT.

Question 77: BPM without end

I have made a BPM. In some cases, if IDocs have not been processed in R3, this BPM will not have an end.

Is there an option that can "kill" this BPM?

A: You can use a deadline branch in which you will have to set your BPM to wait for 24 hours for an example. Inside this deadline branch, you can do something that will finish the BPM:

- Send mail for example that the BPM has finished.
- You can delete the BPM (control step - delete BPM)
- Or throw an exception (control step - throw exception)

Question 78: Monitoring SOAP Message Payload

I am doing a HTTP to SOAP scenario. I want to check if the outgoing payload (after my receiver SOAP adapter finishes processing) is correct.

I tried checking the message in runtime workbench and in message monitor using info from:

https://www.sdn.sap.com/irj/sdn/weblogs?blog=/pub/wlg/1126

And also did this procedure according to:

http://host:port/MessagingSystem/monitor/monitor.jsp

--> Sent Messages / Received Messages --> Sync / Async --> Gave the valid time --> Got a list of messages.

Click on Details --> Display Message Bytes --> Display the entire SOAP message.

The Display Message Bytes displays:

"The message bytes for this synchronous message in final state have been removed from the memory to save resources".

I was able to see the payload for a file scenario (asynchronous). Is there any configuration that I need to do in order to see the payload for a sync call? (LOGGING_SYNC has been set to 1).

A: LOGGING_SYNC is not important with MDT.

You need to set/add in the “Messaging System” in visual admin:

messaging.syncMessageRemover.removeBody = false

Then you will see the payload.

Question 79: Java Proxies and SAP XI Document Problem

I am trying to build the application which is described in the document "Java Proxies and SAP XI Document" Part I and Part II.

https://www.sdn.sap.com/irj/servlet/prt/portal/prtroot/docs/library/uuid/a068cf2f-0401-0010-2aa9-f5ae4b2096f9#search=%22Java%20Proxies%20and%20SAP%20XI%20Document%22

https://www.sdn.sap.com/irj/servlet/prt/portal/prtroot/docs/library/uuid/f272165e-0401-0010-b4a1-e7eb8903501d#search=%22Java%20Proxies%20and%20SAP%20XI%20Document%22

In Part II I have a problem with the code of the InvokeProxy.java. In the Line UsersDBMTResponse_Type response = new UsersDBMTResponse_Type(); "UsersDBMTResponse_Type" can not be resolved. I generated the Java Proxy from IR with both Message Interfaces. Without this java File I can't deploy the whole EJB project. I am using SPS12 and I don't know where my mistake is.

As it seems I already made a mistake in Fig. 5 of this document. I don't know how to make this IM. My IM looks different.

Source Interface: Users_Sync_MI
Target Interface: Users_DB_Sync_MI

Request Tab
Source Message: User_MT
Target Message: Users_DB_MT_response
Mapping Programm: Users_MM

Response Tab
Source Message: Users_DB_MT_response
Target Message: Users_DB_MT
Mapping Programm: Users_resp_MM

Can you help me to reach Fig. 5?

A: You need to first create three message types:

1. User_MT
2. Users_DB_MT
3. Users_DB_MT_response

Create sync o/b interface Users_Sync_MI using output message type User_MT and input message type Users_DB_MT_response.

Create sync i/b interface Users_DB_Sync_MI using input message type Users_DB_MT and output message type Users_DB_MT_response.

Create message mapping as shown in Fig. 3 and Fig. 4.

Question 80: Imported RFC has problem in Converting to XML

I have a RFC with this import parameter from ABAP:

```
data: p_data type tab512 occurs 0.

Call function.......
Tables
DATA = p_data
```

This is the XML source from the mapping test in Int.Rep.

```
<?xml version="1.0" encoding="UTF-8"?>
<ns:Z_BI_SEND_DATA_512 xmlns:ns="urn:sap-com:document:sap:rfc:functions">
<SYSID_HOME>AAA</SYSID_HOME>
<TARGETSYS>BBB</TARGETSYS>
<DATA>
<item>test1</item>
<item>test2</item>
<item>test3</item>
</DATA>
</ns:Z_BI_SEND_DATA_512>
```

This is the payload from SXMB_MONI:


```
<?xml version="1.0" encoding="UTF-8" ?>
- <rfc:Z_BI_SEND_DATA_512 xmlns:rfc="urn:sap-com:document:sap:rfc:functions">
<SYSID_HOME>AAA</SYSID_HOME>
<TARGETSYS>BBB</TARGETSYS>
- <DATA>
- <item>
<WA>test1</WA>
</item>
- <item>
<WA>test2</WA>
</item>
- <item>
<WA>test3</WA>
</item>
</DATA>
</rfc:Z_BI_SEND_DATA_512>
```


Looks like there is a difference (imported RFC in mapping does not show the work area WA) so mapping requires:

```
<DATA>
<item>test1</item>
```

but RFC generates:

```
- <DATA>
- <item>
<WA>test1</WA>
```

Which hinders the mapping from moving the item lines into the destination file because in mapping the WA area cannot be linked as it is not recognized in mapping.

Can you suggest any possible solution to this?

A: Do not forget to activate in SAP BASIS SWCV the element for the substructure "WA" which is the table reference for the data element "item" in your RFC. Then import your RFC again.

Question 81: Problem in Integration Directory after Transport

We did a SLD transport (only LD objects), with DEV and PRD groups. It had some error messages because the SWCVs from the Dev XI were not created into PRD XI. But despite the errors, the products and SWCV's were created.

After that, we've done IR and ID objects transports, through File System. Apparently, the IR part was OK.

In the ID, it correctly changed the Business Systems from Dev Configuration to their respective transport targets. However, if we try to open any Adapter, it gives an error message:

"Attempt to access the 1 requested objects on 1 failed. Detailed information: com.sap.aii.ib.core.roa.RoaObjectAccessException: Unable to read object Adapter Metadata SOAP | http://sap.com/xi/XI/System (b38bcd00-e471-11d7-afac-de420a1145a5) of type AdapterMetaData from application REPOSITORY on system REPOSITORY. Detailed information: Software component version with GUID b38bcd00-e471-11d7-afac-de420a1145a5 does not exist"

We tried to create a new Adapter, but when we get to select adapter type (SOAP, File, RFC, etc.) it says:

"Search Result for All Component Versions
No objects found!"

So, we can't select any adapter type.

Can you help us correct this problem?

A: You need to import the SAP BASIS 6.4 or 7.0 Software Component Version into Integration Repository.

For this ".tpz" file you can get from:

Copy XI3_0_SAP_BASIS_6.40_09_00.tpz from <Components DVD>/XI /XI_CONTENT to directory /usr/sap/<SAPSID>/SYS/global/xi/repository_server/import/

Question 82: SWCV

In a SAP XI .NET scenario, what are the SWCV that has to be imported from SLD?

A: There are no standard software components to be imported from SLD. You need to define what components you will need for your scenario.

Let us say you created a software component SAP_2_NET in SLD; you then will need to import this SWC into repository for implementation in your scenario.

Question 83: Creating a "less than" Condition in the Condition Editor

I'm designing a BPM with a loop which needs to run while a counter is less than a determined value.

I have defined the counter as a simple type container and used a container operator to increment this counter. But in the condition editor for the loop, I did not found a simple way to create this "less than" condition, other than creating a huge OR statement with all the possible values that the counter can assume (1, 2, up to max_value), which I would really rather not to use.

I read about using a XPath expression to create this less than condition, but I need to use it in a simple variable, not a message.

I've also searched through SDN about this, but I didn't manage to find anything on the topic (except for the XPath thing).

Is there any way of doing this?

A: Don't use the "NOT EQUAL TO" in your condition editor.

Initialize the variable to the maximum value and then decrement it. Once it reaches the minimum value for which "NOT EQUAL TO" is defined, it will stop processing and get out of the SWITCH and so on.

The condition editor is used in your BPM only for LOOP (SWITCH STEP).

For additional reference visit:

http://help.sap.com/saphelp_nw04/helpdata/en/67/49767669963545a071a190b77a9a23/content.htm

http://help.sap.com/saphelp_nw04/helpdata/en/ab/13bf7191e73a4fb3560e767a2525fd/content.htm

Question 84: Call the Method on the Object Externally

We have several external non-SAP applications that work online with our SAP system by mean of RFC calls and BAPI calls (using JCO).

BAPI is technically a RFC function, so it makes no difference to the caller that it calls an RFC function or a BAPI. But, a BAPI is also a method on a Business Object.

Is it possible to call the method on the object externally (using JCO or other connector)?

Instead of exposing the implementation of the BAPI (thus the RFC function), I would like to instantiate the Business Object and call its method. Is it possible from outside SAP?

A: No. It is not possible to expose the business object method or its implementation from outside SAP.

A business object method can be implemented in several ways: Function module, API function, Transaction, Dialog module, Report or other.

Thus using JCo or another RFC library should enable you to access the method regarding its implementation.

For implementations of type Report or Transaction this seems very unlikely since a front-end is required.

Question 85: Alert Inbox - One Message

I configured the alert inbox to work. When an error is received, I see it in the alert inbox. However, if another error is received, I don't get any alerts anymore for the same interface.

How do I configure the alert inbox to give an alert for every error?

A: In your ALERT RULE, you must have selected the option,

"SUPRESS MULTIPLE ALERTS OF THIS RULE"

You need to unselect this option, and you will get the alert every time the error occurs for that interface.

Question 86: Calling a RFC from a BPM Process

I have a question about calling a RFC from a BPM process using a synchronous call. When I go to review the graphical workflow log, I can see that the synchronous send task is completed; but when I look at the messages processed by the integration server in SXMB_MONI, I cannot see the successful message sent by my abstract BPM interface. I think that I have all of the receiver determination and interface mappings between the abstract BPM send interface and the inbound RFC interface. The interesting part is that the only time when I can see the message in SXMB_MONI is when I break the interface mapping between the abstract and inbound interfaces.

Do you have any ideas what causes this?

A: You can always see all of the steps of the BMP by clicking PE (in the message monitoring) then "list with technical details" (not the graphical workflow) and then "show item container" on the send step, or mapping, or anything else (the one where you can see all of the XML messages involved).

You can also use TCODE: SXMS_SAMON. It shows the number of active sync calls waiting for a response.

If you have not set logging for synchronous messages, they will not show up in the SXMB_MONI unless they are in error.

To set it up, go to transaction sxmb_adm Configuration, then to “Integration Engine Configuration” then “Change Specific Configuration Data”.

Category : Runtime
Parameter : LOGGING_SYNC
value : 1 (activated)

Question 87: Generic Integration

If you a have a non-SAP system (like Oracle forms based application using oracle DB) that is not SOAP/HTTP/JMS capable how can I have that system push a message out to SAP through XI?

A: Your best option will be to use XI JDBC adapter read a database on that system and send the message to XI.

File and JDBC adapter are the most commonly used. There is also JMS, which is often used with older systems, e.g. mainframe applications, putting messages into a queue which XI will read.

For some systems which are quite common (like Oracle Financials, JDEdwards etc.) 3rd party adapters are available from "Iway" and "Seeburger" mainly. These adapters are sold by SAP and support will also b e provided through SAP OSS. Check out the "Connectivity Section" at:

http://service.sap.com/xi

And then you can always implement a specific adapter if this system has some possibility to extract data, e.g. your own API. IMO is the last resort if you can't use any of the standard adapters, as it requires more effort.

Question 88: Faulty message handling in BPM

I created a business process with a synchronous sending step. I defined all interfaces and implemented an 'own fault message' type within the synchronous abstract interface. If the used RFC got the correct data, the sync sending step works properly and the business process works fine also. If I provide wrong data to the RFC to force it to throw an exception, the 'Business' process receives the fault message.

I just want to send the received fault message asynchronously to a file adapter within the defined exception branch. I was not able to implement a new variable in the container for the fault message type.

How can I send the message?

A: No, you can not send the message. It is definitely not possible to further process the content of the exception message within the exception branch. The exception message received by the BPM only triggers the exception branch. The message itself cannot be defined as an abstract interface.

Question 89: SAP R3 to Legacy System Including Master Data Using XI

I am doing integration from SAP R3 to Legacy system including master data (customer, Material, BOM etc).

Is there any way through an ALE setup that I can send master data (create/change) to Legacy system real time?

A: Yes. This type of scenarios is an R/3->XI->Legacy Systems. In this case R/3 can give the data in different formats either Idoc/RFC/ABAP Proxy. There are some standard IDocs available for this in R/3 (BOM,Material). You can make use of this to configure your IDOC->XI->Legacy System (File) scenario.

The following blog talks about Idoc->XI->File Scenario.

https://www.sdn.sap.com/irj/sdn/weblogs?blog=/pub/wlg/1819

http://help.sap.com/saphelp_nw2004s/helpdata/en/ab/bdb13b00ae793be10000000a11402f/content.htm

When you are talking about Master Data, then you have MDM in your Design. In this case you can use XI for distributing data into legacy systems.

https://www.sdn.sap.com/irj/sdn/weblogs?blog=/pub/wlg/2278

Whenever you change for example PO, data has to automatically update and there are some standard Idocs from SAP (ORDERS, CHNG). Whenever it triggers that Idoc, you need to make sure that it should reach XI. For this, you need to fill control record information like logical system, port etc. This scenario is of adHoc type. You can even schedule the Idoc processing once in a day, etc.

Check this SAP help.

http://help.sap.com/saphelp_erp2004/helpdata/en/dc/6b8359 43d711d1893e0000e8323c4f/content.htm

http://www.netweaverguru.com/EDI/HTML/IDocBook.htm

http://help.sap.com/saphelp_nw2004s/helpdata/en/0b/2a65ec 507d11d18ee90000e8366fc2/frameset.htm

For Proxy you can schedule the ABAP report so that it will send the message to XI. You can write a small ABAP report from there which you can call "RFC/ABAP proxy/BAPI ".

If you define proper logical systems/RFC destinations, then message will reach XI.

http://help.sap.com/saphelp_nw2004s/helpdata/en/02/265c3c f311070ae10000000a114084/content.htm

Question 90: Webservice

I am working on a Webservice scenario. I created a RFC function module and converted the same to Webservice. But while creating communication channels, I need to pass the target URL.

I passed the URL location, but I got the following error message:


```
******************
<?xml version="1.0" encoding="UTF-8" standalone="yes" ?>
- <!-- Call Adapter
-->
- <SAP:Error xmlns:SAP="http://sap.com/xi/XI/Message/30"
xmlns:SOAP="http://schemas.xmlsoap.org/soap/envelope/"
SOAP:mustUnderstand="1">
<SAP:Category>XIAdapter</SAP:Category>
<SAP:Code
area="PARSING">ADAPTER.SOAP_EXCEPTION</SAP:Code>
<SAP:P1 />
<SAP:P2 />
<SAP:P3 />
<SAP:P4 />
<SAP:AdditionalText>soap fault: SOAP processing failure, error id =
1001</SAP:AdditionalText>
<SAP:ApplicationFaultMessage namespace="" />
<SAP:Stack />
<SAP:Retry>M</SAP:Retry>
</SAP:Error>
***************
```


Can you help me solve this problem?

A: The information below will surely help you find an answer.

If you are on WAS 6.20 and up, you can expose an RFC as a webservice directly from WAS.

If you're on Basis layer 4.6D, you will need to use XI (or some other integration tool) to expose the RFC as a webservice.

To do this in XI you'll need to do the following:

Integration Repository

1. Import the RFC.
2. Define a message and datatype for the SOAP interface.
3. Create inbound and outbound interfaces.
4. Create maps between the RFC and SOAP messages.
5. Create an interface map.

Integration Directory

1. Create an RFC Receiver Channel.
2. Create a SOAP Sender Channel.
3. Generate the WSDL (Tools->Define Web Service).

You can then handoff the WSDL and a login username and password to your dev eloper and they will have everything they need to make the WS call.

Here are answers to a few questions that might arise.

1. Do I need to actually create a WS that calls the RFC? Isn't the virtual interface exposed by the XI sufficient?

   Yes, you need to create a WS in XI that calls the RFC.

2. If I really have to create the WS and deploy it in order to expose it with the XI, then what is my benefit of exposing it with the XI? Why not just expose it as a normal WS?

   You don't have WAS 6.20 or up. Even if you did, you may still want to expose it using XI in order to have all of your integration go through the same application.

3. If I expose my web service through the XI, how does the client application executes one of its methods? To which url does it have to access (the XI or the actual WS)?

   You expose a SOAP interface in XI by generating a WSDL file. This file contains all of the information a developer will need to call the webservice including the URL.

   You actually specify the URL when you generate the WSDL. Be sure to read the documentation to get the correct format because the URL that the wizard suggests isn't correct.

Question 91: Polling Interval

How do you set a polling interval, in case of IDoc to file scenario ? How about in other scenarios?

A: There is actually no need to set a polling interval for an IDoc to file scenario . Interval/s will be set when you need to pick the file and sent into XI, for example, when your scenario is like File to XI to IDoc/RFC etc.

In your IDoc to File scenario, your IDoc will be triggered from your external system, and there is no sender IDoc adapter, so there is obviously no polling interval for the same.

In the case of your file, as the file adapter is a receiver file adapter, it will generate your file whenever the IDoc is triggered from your external system and so no polling interval is also required for the receiver file adapter.

For how to do an IDoc to File scenario, refer to this blog:

https://weblogs.sdn.sap.com/pub/wlg/1819

In the case of File to XI to IDoc, the polling interval will have to be specified in your File Adapter. Now, the interval to be mentioned depends on how often you want the file adapter to scan and search for files.

If you say, 10 seconds, then the adapter will poll every 10 seconds for the file. So, the poll interval you give will be purely on how often the file is to be picked by XI and passed as an IDoc to the external system.

In the case of a File to IDoc scenario, The XI Sender File Adapter picks up the file to send to the target/receiving system. The Sender File Adapter can be configured to poll at regular intervals. The polling interval can be set as per the schedule of the extract program. In case the extract is on-demand, then you can set the polling interval to 60 secs or 600 secs. The point is that the interface can be triggered by the File Adapter polling mechanism.

There are a few parameters which you define while configuring the Sender File/FTP Adapter, so I thought I will just tell you what exactly a few of them relating to polling time mean:

1. Poll Interval (secs) - Number of seconds that the adapter must wait if no files are found for processing.

2. Poll Interval (msecs) - Additional waiting time in milliseconds.

    a. If Poll Interval (secs) is set to null, processing times will be short and close to real time.
    b. If Poll Interval (secs) and Poll Interval (msecs) are set to null, the adapter is only called once.

3. Retry Interval (secs) - Specify the number of seconds that the adapter is to wait before a file processed with errors is processed again.

    a. If the value is set to null, then the adapter is canceled if an error occurs, even if a value greater than null is specified for Poll Interval (secs).

While configuring a sender file adapter, a major mistake that we often do is keeping file adapter communication channel polling interval less and in test mode. It is not an error, keeping it in test mode with less polling interval but, often we forget about it, keeping the adapter channel active and it loads the server memory unnecessarily.

The link below will help you understand things better.

http://help.sap.com/saphelp_nw04/helpdata/en/e3/94007075cae04f930cc4c034e411e1/frameset.htm

http://help.sap.com/saphelp_nw04/helpdata/en/03/80a74052033713e10000000a155106/frameset.htm

http://help.sap.com/saphelp_nw04/helpdata/en/17/7481b6d5095b42bd804d1815201ebc/frameset.htm

Question 92: JDBC Java SQL Exception Error

I got the following SQL error for the JDBC adapter.

TransformException error in xml processor class: Error processing request in sax parser: Error when executing statement for table/stored proc. 'CUSTOMER' (structure 'statementname'): java.sql.SQLException: [SQL7008] TEST1 in QGPL not valid for operation.

The following is the XML message payload:

<?xml version="1.0" encoding="utf-8" ?>
- <ns1:TESTCUSTOMER xmlns:ns1="http://test.com/xi/JDBC">
- <statementname>
- <CUSTOMER action="insert">
- <access>
<TEST1>100</TEST1>
</access>
</CUSTOMER>
</statementname>
</ns1:TESTCUSTOMER>

CUSTOMER is the name of the TABLE. TEST1 is a column existing in the table.

We wrote a JAVA programmed to insert the data into the table using the same JDBC driver and it worked fine.

Can you help me make this work?

A: Use this setting to see the SQL coming out of your adapter, refer to note: 801367 .

JDBC Receiver Adapter Parameters:

1. Parameter name: "logSQLStatement"
Parameter type: boolean

Parameter value: true for any string value, false only for empty string

Parameter value default: false (empty String)

Available with: SP9

Category: 2

Description:

When implementing a scenario with the JDBC receiver adapter, it may be helpful to see which SQL statement is generated by the JDBC adapter from the XI message content for error analysis. Before SP9, this can only be found in the trace of the JDBC adapter if trace level DEBUG is activated. With SP9, the generated SQL statement will be shown in the details page (audit protocol) of the message monitor for each message directly.

This should be used only during the test phase and not in productive scenarios.

The error was due to the commit in the database. You did not use any parameters in the Advance Mode.

Question 93: Problem with BPM Starting

I defined a BPM Object. Message has been received correctly, but no instances of the BPM have been started. I simulated the same BPM with another old XI System and it works.

The error is an "Outbound Error" in the monitor (red flag).

What can be the cause of this and how do I solve it?

A: You will need to check up SXI_CACHE to see if your BPM is enabled. See what the return code is; it should be "0". If the value is not "0", try activating BPM from there.

Question 94: Sales Document Type not defined

I am working on an interface, which is designed as follows.

Purchase Order->File Adapter->XI (BPM) ->RFC Adapter->Sales Order in R/3

When I tried to create a sales document in R/3, I got a message back from R/3 saying "Sales Document is not defined", but when checked in R/3, that sales document type exist. I don't see any mapping exception in monitoring.

I used a standard BAPI called BAPI_SALESORDER_PROXY_CREATE for sales order creation. In my input xml file, I have a value for a field called 'DocTypeCode' as 'Z4OR'. I ran the test even without this filed value and it gave me the same message.

Initially it was a value-mapping problem.

Is it possible to debug a BAPI /RFC from XI?

If it is possible, please advise me of the procedure. My XI is working fine but I am getting a message back from R/3 as follows:


```
<?xml version="1.0" encoding="UTF-8" ?>
- <rfc:BAPI_SALESORDER_PROXY_CREATE.Response
xmlns:rfc="urn:sap-com:document:sap:rfc:functions">
<E_SALESDOCUMENT_EX />
<E_STATUS>E</E_STATUS>
- <RETURN>
- <item>
<TYPE>S</TYPE>
<ID>V4</ID>
<NUMBER>233</NUMBER>
<MESSAGE>SALES_HEADER_IN has been processed
successfully</MESSAGE>
<LOG_NO />
<LOG_MSG_NO>000000</LOG_MSG_NO>
<MESSAGE_V1>VBAKKOM</MESSAGE_V1>
<MESSAGE_V2 />
<MESSAGE_V3 />
<MESSAGE_V4 />
<PARAMETER>SALES_HEADER_IN</PARAMETER>
<ROW>0</ROW>
<FIELD />
<SYSTEM>UD1CLNT010</SYSTEM>
</item>
- <item>
<TYPE>E</TYPE>
<ID>V1</ID>
<NUMBER>384</NUMBER>
<MESSAGE>Sales unit ****** is not defined for item
000000</MESSAGE>
<LOG_NO />
<LOG_MSG_NO>000000</LOG_MSG_NO>
<MESSAGE_V1>******</MESSAGE_V1>
<MESSAGE_V2>000000</MESSAGE_V2>
<MESSAGE_V3 />
<MESSAGE_V4 />
<PARAMETER>SALES_ITEM_IN</PARAMETER>
<ROW>1</ROW>
<FIELD />
<SYSTEM>UD1CLNT010</SYSTEM>
```

```
</item>
- <item>
<TYPE>E</TYPE>
<ID>V4</ID>
<NUMBER>248</NUMBER>
<MESSAGE>Error in SALES_ITEM_IN 000001</MESSAGE>
<LOG_NO />
<LOG_MSG_NO>000000</LOG_MSG_NO>
<MESSAGE_V1>VBAPKOM</MESSAGE_V1>
<MESSAGE_V2>000001</MESSAGE_V2>
<MESSAGE_V3 />
<MESSAGE_V4 />
<PARAMETER>SALES_ITEM_IN</PARAMETER>
<ROW>1</ROW>
<FIELD />
<SYSTEM>UD1CLNT010</SYSTEM>
</item>
- <item>
<TYPE>E</TYPE>
<ID>V4</ID>
<NUMBER>219</NUMBER>
<MESSAGE>Sales document was not changed</MESSAGE>
<LOG_NO />
<LOG_MSG_NO>000000</LOG_MSG_NO>
<MESSAGE_V1 />
<MESSAGE_V2>000001</MESSAGE_V2>
<MESSAGE_V3 />
<MESSAGE_V4 />
<PARAMETER />
<ROW>0</ROW>
<FIELD />
<SYSTEM>UD1CLNT010</SYSTEM>
</item>
- <item>
<TYPE>E</TYPE>
<ID>C_</ID>
<NUMBER>005</NUMBER>
<MESSAGE>The object references could not be written to the CRMKEY</MESSAGE>
<LOG_NO />
<LOG_MSG_NO>000000</LOG_MSG_NO>
<MESSAGE_V1 />
<MESSAGE_V2 />
```

```
<MESSAGE_V3 />
<MESSAGE_V4 />
<PARAMETER />
<ROW>0</ROW>
<FIELD />
<SYSTEM>UD1CLNT010</SYSTEM>
</item>
</RETURN>
<TI_EXTENSIONIN />
<TI_ORDER_CCARD />
<TI_ORDER_CFGS_BLOB />
<TI_ORDER_CFGS_INST />
<TI_ORDER_CFGS_PART_OF />
<TI_ORDER_CFGS_REF />
<TI_ORDER_CFGS_REFINST />
<TI_ORDER_CFGS_VALUE />
<TI_ORDER_CFGS_VK />
- <TI_ORDER_CONDITIONS_IN>
- <item>
<ITM_NUMBER>000001</ITM_NUMBER>
<COND_ST_NO>000</COND_ST_NO>
<COND_COUNT>00</COND_COUNT>
<COND_TYPE>EDI1</COND_TYPE>
<COND_VALUE>57.600000000</COND_VALUE>
<CURRENCY>AUD</CURRENCY>
<COND_UNIT />
<COND_P_UNT>1</COND_P_UNT>
<CURR_ISO />
<CD_UNT_ISO />
<REFOBJTYPE />
<REFOBJKEY />
<REFLOGSYS />
<APPLICATIO />
```


A: You can't debug an R/3 RFC from XI. This looks like a data problem based on message: <MESSAGE>Sales unit ****** is not defined for item 000000</MESSAGE>

The UOM you are sending in for the material is not valid.

You will need to remove the UOM from the input xml instance and pass the data through.

Question 95: Global Data Types

We have complex types that we would like to use across software components. I want to create a data type which references a data type outside the current SWC.

Is this possible?

A: Yes, it is possible. I just tested one a few weeks ago. Let me explain with an example:

SWC:A (contains the data type which you want to reference, say, include_DT)
SWC:B (contains the data type where you want to reference a DT which is in SWC:A. Lets call it Main_DT).

You need to create the dependency between SWC:A and SWC:B in the SLD.

While creating the Main_DT, you will have to use "Search Help" to reference the include_DT in any of the sub-elements that you have. But you cannot reference the include_DT at the root element level in Main_DT.

Question 96: IDoc to R/3

I need to check the IDoc sent from XI to R/3. I need to see the results and verify if there are any errors.

How can I do this?

A: You need to go to transaction we02/we05. On the left of the screen, double click on the IDoc type that you sent. A list of transactions will be displayed; check the IDoc corresponding to your scenario, and check if it is green.

Sm58 is the tRFC queue and check if there are some entries. Only errors are recorded there. If there is no entry for your IDoc here, then, your scenario is successful.

You may want to take a look at this link. It will help you understand where you can look if an error occurred.

http://help.sap.com/saphelp_nw04/helpdata/en/6a/e6194119d8f323e10000000a155106/frameset.htm

Question 97: "Scheduled for outbound processing" Message

My scenario is:

R/3 (IDoc Customer) -> XI -> PC (file)

I use a BPM with option "multi to single".

In the Message Monitoring, I have two steps:

1. Idoc DEBMAS06 --> BPM: status = "Processed successfully".
2. BPM --> my PC: status = "Scheduled for Outbound processing" and in column "outbound" I have not "IENGINE". There is no other error message and obviously no data are sent to my PC.

I have checked transaction SMQ2. I can see that queue status = "SYSFAIL" and I have two type of message:

- XI Error CLIENT_RECEIVE_FAILED.INTERNAL: Queue stop
- XI restart in qRFC not allowed.

Can you help me sort this out?

A: Yes. First, reset the status to "Ready".

Then if you get SYSFAIL again, delete that particular LUW. If there are other messages waiting in the queue, just click on the unlockqueue button and the remaining messages will flow thru.

Question 98: Conversion Agent - Integration with XI / SP15

We are trying to evaluate the features of the Conversion Agent and its usage within XI / SP15 (Windows based).

We did the first CA HL7 tutorial and deployed the correct transformation script as Conversion Agent "Service" named "HL7_Parsing_Test". When we tried to run the Service via the "CM_Console", everything was passed successfully.

However, when we tried to include the service in our File Sender Adapter which parses the same HL7 source file, we got a "NullPointerException" (and the File Sender Adapter went to red light).

We added the Conversion Agent "CMTransformBean" to our communication channel and set the parameter "TransformationName" to the value "HL7_Parsing_Test" without success.

The exact configuration is as follows:

1. Added Modulname: "localejbs/sap.com/com.sap.nw.cm.xi/CMTransformBean" (JNDI-Name of CMTransformBean). Type of Bean = "Local Enterprise Bean"
2. Parametername: "TransformationName"
3. Parameter value: "HL7_Parsing_Test"

How do you successfully include the CMtransformBean into an XI communication channel?

A: You need to check whether you added the CMtransformBean before the CallSapAdapter Bean in the module chain, and not after it. Placing the CMtransformBean after the CallSapAdapter Bean causes the above error that you encountered.

Question 99: Soap Error: Content-Type of the Request should be Text/XML

I am working on a HTTP-SOAP scenario and I have checked the "Do not use SOAP Envelope" check box, in the receiver soap adapter. I created the message payload with the SOAP envelope in the interface mapping.

When I sent a request to the webservice, I got the following error:

```
<faultcode>soapenv:Client</faultcode>
<faultstring>content-type of the request should be
text/xml</faultstring>
```

When I checked the message payload in MDT, I found that an extra soap envelope is added by the adapter in spite of the setting made in the receiver soap adapter. This extra soap envelope has content-type as application/xml and hence the error.

Here is the payload:

```
--SAP_3c63dd11-369b-11db-902c-0002559ad50b_END
Content-ID: <soap-3c63dd10369b11dba74e0002559ad50b@sap.com>
Content-Disposition: attachment;filename="soap-
3c63dd10369b11dba74e0002559ad50b@sap.com.xml"
Content-Type: text/xml; charset=utf-8
Content-Description: SOAP

--------Begin of extra soap envelope--------

<SOAP:Envelope
xmlns:SOAP='http://schemas.xmlsoap.org/soap/envelope/'>
<SOAP:Header xmlns:xlink='http://www.w3.org/1999/xlink'
xmlns:SAP='http://sap.com/xi/XI/Message/30'
xmlns:wsse='http://www.docs.oasis-open.org/wss/2004/01/oasis-
200401-wss-wssecurity-secext-1.0.xsd'>
<SAP:Main versionMajor='3' versionMinor='0'
SOAP:mustUnderstand='1' xmlns:wsu='http://www.docs.oasis-
open.org/wss/2004/01/oasis-200401-wss-wssecurity-utility-1.0.xsd'
wsu:Id='wsuid-main-92ABE13F5C59AB7FE10000000A1551F7'>
```

```
<SAP:MessageClass>ApplicationMessage</SAP:MessageClass>
<SAP:ProcessingMode>synchronous</SAP:ProcessingMode>
<SAP:MessageId>44f2ef85-b9e1-0045-0000-
000091 1aa04f</SAP:MessageId>
<SAP:TimeSent>2006-08-28T13:43:28Z</SAP:TimeSent>
<SAP:Sender><SAP:Party agency=" scheme="></SAP:Party>
<SAP:Service>HTTPSENDER</SAP:Service>
</SAP:Sender>
<SAP:Receiver><SAP:Party agency=" scheme=">
</SAP:Party><SAP:Service>SOAPRECEIVER</SAP:Service></SAP:
Receiver><SAP:Interface
namespace='urn:horizon:sforce'>MI_SFORCE</SAP:Interface></SAP:
Main><SAP:ReliableMessaging
SOAP:mustUnderstand='1'><SAP:QualityOfService>BestEffort</SAP:
QualityOfService></SAP:ReliableMessaging><SAP:Diagnostic
SOAP:mustUnderstand='1'><SAP:TraceLevel>Fatal</SAP:TraceLevel
><SAP:Logging>Off</SAP:Logging></SAP:Diagnostic><SAP:HopLi
st SOAP:mustUnderstand='1'><SAP:Hop timeStamp='2006-08-
28T13:43:28Z' wasRead='false'><SAP:Engine
type='IS'></SAP:Engine><SAP:Adapter
namespace='http://sap.com/xi/XI/System'>HTTP</SAP:Adapter><SA
P:MessageId>44f2ef85-b9e1-0045-0000-
000091 1aa04f</SAP:MessageId><SAP:Info>host:ztm0042.services.sh
ell.net:8005::remote-
addr:145.30.233.51</SAP:Info></SAP:Hop><SAP:Hop
timeStamp='2006-08-28T13:43:28Z' wasRead='false'><SAP:Engine
type='IS'>is.05.ztm0042</SAP:Engine><SAP:Adapter
namespace='http://sap.com/xi/ XI/System'>XI</SAP:Adapter><SAP:M
essageId>44f2ef85-b9e1-0045-0000-
000091 1aa04f</SAP:MessageId><SAP:Info>3.0</SAP:Info></SAP:H
op><SAP:Hop timeStamp='2006-08-28T13:43:30Z'
wasRead='false'><SAP:Engine
type='AE'>af.dx5.ztm0042</SAP:Engine><SAP:Adapter
namespace='http://sap.com/xi/XI/System'>XIRA</SAP:Adapter><SAP
:MessageId>44f2ef85-b9e1-0045-0000-
000091 1aa04f</SAP:MessageId></SAP:Hop></SAP:HopList></SOA
P:Header><SOAP:Body><sap:Manifest
xmlns:sap='http://sap.com/xi/XI/Message/30'
xmlns:xlink='http://www.w3.org/1999/xlink'
xmlns:wsu='http://www.docs.oasis-open.org/wss/2004/01/oasis-
200401-wss-wssecurity-utility-1.0.xsd' wsu:Id='wsuid-manifest-
5CABE13F5C59AB7FE10000000A1551F7'><sap:Payload
xlink:type='simple' xlink:href='cid:payload-
```

```
44F2EF86B9E1004500000000911AA04F@sap.com'><sap:Name>MainDocument</sap:Name><sap:Description></sap:Description><sap:Type>Application</sap:Type></sap:Payload></sap:Manifest></SOAP:Body></SOAP:Envelope>
--SAP_3c63dd11-369b-11db-902c-0002559ad50b_END
content-id: payload-
44F2EF86B9E1004500000000911AA04F@sap.com
content-type: application/xml;charset=UTF-8
```

------End of extra soap envelope-----------

------Below is the expected payload, generated using xsl--

```
<?xml version="1.0" encoding="utf-8"?>
<soap:Envelope
xmlns:soap="http://schemas.xmlsoap.org/soap/envelope/"
xmlns:xsi="http://www.w3.org/2001/XMLSchema-instance"
xmlns:xsd="http://www.w3.org/2001/XMLSchema">
<soap:Body>
<ns1:login xmlns:ns1="urn:enterprise.soap.sforce.com">
<ns1:username>apiabc</ns1:username>
<ns1:password>123</ns1:password>
</ns1:login>
</soap:Body>
</soap:Envelope>

--SAP_3c63dd11-369b-11db-902c-0002559ad50b_END—
```

Can you give any help on this?

A: Yes. You need to add "&nosoap=true" in the receiver soap adapter target URL.

Question 100: Problem Exporting XML via RFC

I used RFC to send XML data from CRM to XI. My function module (/MARS/CPE_IMPORT_CRM_CATALOG) contains only one parameter (IV_CATALOG) declared as a string so all XML data is placed in this string.

I tried sending the following string from CRM:

<TEST>GREG</TEST>

The payload on XI looks like this:

<xml version="1.0" encoding="UTF-8"?>
<rfc:_-MARS_-CPE_IMPORT_CRM_CATALOG
xmlns:rfc="urn:sap-com:document:sap:rfc:functions">
<IV_CATALOG><TEST>GREG</TEST></IV_C
ATALOG></rfc:_-MARS_-CPE_IMPORT_CRM_CATALOG>

We can see < is converted into < and > into >

Where and how do I specify that the content of the parameter must not be interpreted?

A: The RFC adapter serializes the content of the parameters (for instance the characters < and >) in order to avoid conflicts with real XML tags, as you can easily create non valid XML.

Add the following mapping between the adapter andyour real mapping. This mapping simply converts the < resp. > into < resp. >. It is then possible to send XML into the RFC parameters. If the XML sent in the parameter is not well formed, the message will be rejected by XI.

```
package com.sap.mymappings;

import java.io.BufferedReader;
import java.io.IOException;
import java.io.InputStream;
import java.io.InputStreamReader;
import java.io.OutputStream;
import java.util.Map;

import com.sap.aii.mapping.api.StreamTransformation;

public class DecodeXml implements StreamTransformation {
private Map map;
private OutputStream out;

/**
*
*/
public DecodeXml() {
super();
// Auto-generated constructor stub
}

/**
* method setParamters is required, but we do not anything with it
*/
public void setParameter(Map param) {
map = param;
}

/**
* method execute is called by the XI mapping program
*/
public void execute(InputStream in, OutputStream out)
throws com.sap.aii.mapping.api.StreamTransformationException {
InputStreamReader inReader = new InputStreamReader(in);
```

```
// 2. Helper classes to read in data
BufferedReader bufReader = new BufferedReader(inReader);
String s;
String helpString = new String();
String resString = new String();

int i = 0;
try {
while ((s = bufReader.readLine()) != null) {
helpString = s.replaceAll("&#60;", "<");
helpString = helpString.replaceAll("&#62;", ">");
resString = resString + helpString;
i++;
}
} catch (IOException e) {
// TODO Auto-generated catch block
e.printStackTrace();
}
try {
bufReader.close();
} catch (IOException e1) {
// TODO Auto-generated catch block
e1.printStackTrace();
}

// 4. Write data to OutputStream
byte[] resByte = resString.getBytes();
try {
out.write(resByte, 0, resByte.length);
} catch (IOException e2) {
// TODO Auto-generated catch block
e2.printStackTrace();
}

}
}
```

Acknowledgements:

https://www.sdn.sap.com/irj/sdn/collaboration

http://help.sap.com/saphelp_nw04/helpdata/en/14/80243b4a66ae0ce10000000a11402f/frameset.htm

http://en.wikipedia.org/wiki/SAP-XI

Reviewers

SAPCOOKBOOK would like to acknowledge the kind efforts of several XI experts who have reviewed the manuscript. Only one reviewer returned any feedback whatsoever.

Acronyms:

ABAP - Advanced Business Application Programming
BAPI - Business Application Programming Interface
BPM - Business Process Management
CC - Communication Channel
CMS - Change Management Service
LUW - Logical Units of Work
NWDS - NetWeaver Developer Studio
OSS - Online Service System
RFC - Remote Function Call
RWB – Runtime Workbench
SLD - System Landscape Directory
SOAP - Simple Object Access Protocol (XML protocol)
SSL – Secured Socket Layer
SWCV - Software Component Versions
UME - User Management Engine
UOM - Unit Of Measure
VPN - Virtual Private Network
WSDL - Web Services Description Language (XML format)
XML - Extensible Markup Language
XSLT - Extensible Stylesheet Language Transformations

INDEX

www.ingramcontent.com/pod-product-compliance
Lightning Source LLC
LaVergne TN
LVHW042336060326
832902LV00006B/195

* 9 7 8 1 9 3 3 8 0 4 6 8 2 *